QUALITY MANAGEMENT PRACTICES IN INDIAN MANUFACTURING ORGANISATIONS

QUALITY MANAGEMENT PRACTICES IN INDIAN MANUFACTURING ORGANISATIONS

KARUNESH SAXENA
(M.B.A., Ph.D.)

Ess Ess Publications

4837/24, ANSARI ROAD, DARYA GANJ
NEW DELHI-110002
Phone : 3260807

First Published 1997

ISBN : 81-7000-191-9

Rs. 225/-

Published by
Ess Ess Publications
4837/24, Ansari Road, Darya Ganj
New Delhi-110 002 Ph. 3260807

Composed by
Classic Computer Services
RZ 128/6K Lane No. 9 East Sagar Pur,
New Delhi-110 046 Ph. 5529455

Printed at: Mehra Offset Press

CONTENTS

PREFACE

As early as in the time of construction of Egyptian pyramids, conscious efforts for Quality Control were visible. The subject discipline has come a long way since then.

The globalisation of market emphasises the necessity for Indian Business Organisations, both in public and private sector to produce quality goods and services, in order to survive and prosper. The inevitable entry of multinational corporations has threatened their Indian counterparts to wakeup to the increasing quality needs of the new breed of customers. There has been thrust on management of quality system in recent times which attempts to control the quality levels of entire production process. Quality Management recognises the importance of broad systems issues and seeks effective ways of integrating the large number of people with large number of machines and huge quantities of information.

Increased attention is being paid by the authorities on the subject to the different aspects of Quality Management such as, Development of the principles of Quality Management, Change in Management culture and attitudes, implementation of Quality improvement process etc. The need for studying **Quality Management Practices** over a cross section of the industries is acutely felt because of the advent of global quality standards.

The present study is concerned with the subject area of the Quality Management. The study has been made to explore the current Quality Management Practices prevalent in industrial organisations of Madhya Pradesh.

The book is organised into six chapters. Chapter 1 throws light on introduction of the topic. Discussions on various definitions of Quality, historical evolution of Quality, Organisation for Quality Management have been incorporated. A section on ISO 9000 series and Quality Management has been included in this chapter. The progress made by Indian organisations, with respect to ISO 9000 certification, has been sketched.

In chapter 2 relevant literature has been reviewed. Sections on factors of Quality Management, Quality and Productivity have been made. A section has been devoted to review of empirical studies on world wide Quality Management Practices. Finally the literature available on Indian studies conducted in this subject area, has been reviewed.

Chapter 3 is concerned with Research Methodology. Rationale of the study has been given first, followed by statement of the problem, scope and objectives of the study. A section on operational definitions relevant to the present study has been given, followed by sections on research design, procedure of sampling and data collection. The development of an instrument to measure Quality Management Practices has been described. The brief description of the questionnaire, analysis scheme, and limitations of the study have been dealt with.

In chapter 4 appropriate statistical tools have been applied to systematically analyse the collected data. The sample profile, analysis of Quality Management Practices instrument, development of Quality Management Practices Index, and influence of organisation characteristics on Quality Management Practices have been included in this chapter. Chapter 5 deals with analysing the impact of Organisational environmental factors on Quality Management Practices.

Against the backdrop of the study the author has developed perspective on Quality Management Practices, which is included in Chapter 6. A macro level view point has been develop for improving Quality Management Practices. In the end suggestions for further research have been given.

In Appendix, questionnaire, list of participating organisations, their QMP scores, analysis tables and bibliography have been included.

The study assumes significance in the light of liberalisation measures taken up by the government as a result the level of competition is increasing and weightage is being given to improve the quality of products. The researcher's efforts would be amply rewarded if this study proves to be helpful in field applications.

31st October, 1995. **KARUNESH SAXENA**

ACKNOWLEDGEMENT

First of all, I offer my heartfelt respect and gratitude to my respected teacher **Prof. R.K. Jain**, Faculty of Management Studies, Vikram University, Ujjain for his consistent guidance and encouragement. Without his deep insight into the subject, the study would not have taken its present shape.

Prof. Nageshwar Rao, Director, Pt. Jawaharlal Nehru Institute of Business Management has extended all possible help and encouragement. I offer my deeply felt gratitude to him.

All the members of **JNIBM family** have contributed immensely towards completion of this study. My colleagues, Dr. P.K. Sharma, Dr. Ravindra Jain, Dr. R.P. Das, Dr. Deepak Gupta, Mr. Sanjay Dubey, Mr. P.K. Singh and Dr. D. Meena have provided cooperation and moral support. I would like to express my sincere thanks to all of them. From the supporting staff Miss Sandhya Saxena, Dr. Kaushik Bose, Mr. Rakesh Khoti and Mrs. Suneeta Singh have been very helpful. I thank them very much for their efforts. Dr. Man Singh Gurjar, Lecturer, School of Studies in Political Science, has been a constant source of inspiration to me. I offer my gratitude to him.

My friends Mr. Kishore Katthar, A.E., M.P.E.B., Indore; Mr. P.P.S. Chawla, Inspector, Central Excise, Indore; Mr. T. Alex John, Executive Officer to the M.D., OPTEL, Bhopal; Mr. Rajneesh Chaudhary, Drug Inspector, Dewas and

Mr. Vedvrat Singh Bais, Research Associate, Barkatullah University, Bhopal; have helped me a lot in data collection activities.

My students deserve special appreciation for their cooperation. All the executives who participated in this study deserve special recognition. I thank them all because without their support this study would not have been completed.

Mr. K.K. Saxena and Mr. S.K. Saxena of PICK Computers and Mr. V.K. Saxena of Computer Center, Vikram University provided immense help in analysis of data and meticulous processing of the manuscript.

Mrs. Sheel Sethi and Mr. Sumit Sethi of Ess Ess Publications have been very enthusiastic and encouraging. Excellent quality of production of this book is attributable to their enthusiasm. Mr. Ravinder Kumar of Classic Computer Services has been innovative and instrumental in giving the book its present shape. My heart felt thanks are due to all of them.

All my family members encouraged me for completing this study. My father in law **Dr. K.K. Verma** has helped me in all stages of this study. The present book is possible due to the blessings given by my elder brother **Dr. Kamlesh Saxena.** I express my deep sense of respect and gratitude to all of them.

Finally my wife **Dr. Rashmi Saxena** has made painstaking efforts for bringing this book to its satisfactory completion. Without her patience and persistence, this book would not have seen the light of the day.

KARUNESH SAXENA

LIST OF TABLES

CHAPTER 1

QUALITY MANAGEMENT : EVOLUTION AND CONCEPT

Every act by an organisation to ensure that a product or service meets a desired or specified standard comes under the purview of quality control activity. Quality control is almost as old as the human race. In the ancient times the quality control activity was not performed consciously but was part of every day activities. In recent times quality control has emerged as a primary function in business organisations. It is attributed to various factors such as rapid industrial growth, specialisation of labour, technological advancements, precision in and complexity of production, increased consumer awareness, and stiff competitive environment.

Due to the recent economic liberalisation measures of the Government, new vistas of international competition have opened up. The globalisation of market emphasises the necessity for Indian business organisations to produce quality goods and services, in order to survive and prosper. The inevitable entry of Multi National Corporations has threatened their Indian counterparts to wake up to the increasing quality needs of the new breed of customers, who are basking in the safety of protection of consumer rights. As a result, many Indian business organisations are experiencing a renaissance. In the wake of increased competition business organisations adopt a strategic attitude where in quality improvement is emphasised.

HISTORICAL EVOLUTION OF QUALITY

As early as in the time of construction of Egyptian pyramids, conscious efforts at quality control were visible. The ancient Romans developed high-quality reinforced concrete in structural engineering. The excellent quality of roads, bridges, orderly design of cities in to blocks, bear testimony to this fact.

In the middle ages the quality standards were self-established as the individual was both the producer and the inspector.

Craft guilds were formed which are medieval associations of master craftsmen in Europe. In their efforts to manage quality, the guilds set standards for the quality of goods (Encyclopedia Americana, 1985).

Towards the end of nineteenth century the 'Journal of American Statistical Society' began its publication, which provided a source of current technical developments in the field of quality and reliability. With the onset of twentieth century the era of supervisor has begun as the need was felt to form group of workers. In 1924 the western electric bell telephone laboratory pioneered to form the Inspection Engineering Department. The credit for doing the pioneering work in the field of Quality Control goes to H.F. Dodge, D.A. Quarles, W.A. Shewhart, G.D. Edwards, Harry G. Romig and others. This group worked for Weston Electric's Bell Telephone Laboratories during the period 1924-27. Their important contributions include Shewhart Control Charts, various terms associated with acceptance sampling, Dodge's acceptance sampling by attributes. In 1925, the basic concepts of sampling inspection by attributes were given by Dodge. The Western Electric group's Inspection Engineering Department gave the concepts of Average Outgoing Quality Level (AOQL), sampling tables, and the concept of multiple sampling.

By 1930's the pioneering work which was being carried out at Western Electric's spread to the other industrial organisations both in the United States and abroad. Scanlon put forward the concept of quality control through employee motivation and involvement, that was called the 'Scanlon plan'. This plan proposed, in essence, the employees, supervisors and managers to work unitedly for improving the overall quality of work life (Feigenbaum, 1983). Jennet and Welch (1939) wrote the article entitled "The control of production Defective as judged by a Single Quality Characteristic varying on a continuous scale", which laid the foundation of variable sampling.

In 1940/s the berth of statistical quality control. Dodge and Romig present (Lot Tolerance Percent Defective) protection sampling scheme based on fixed consumer's risk, which led to the Dodge-Romig system. These schemes were disseminated in the published form through an article (Dodge & Romig, 1941) and also in book form in 1944 (Dodge & Romig, 1944). It has come to be known as the Dodge-Romig System. (They also offered AOQL (Average Outgoing Quality Level) protection schemes consisting of rectifying inspection plans that guaranteed some stated protection after 100% inspection of rejected lots.)

Due to the second world war the rapid expansion had taken place in industries connected with war-time materials. Greater emphasis was laid on the quality related aspects of these goods, for obvious reasons. During this period the need was felt for having nationally and internationally accredited laboratories to give honest, accurate and precise laboratory evaluations or certifications (Banks, 1989).

In 1950's various quality control standards were developed and modified. Around the same time the concept of quality control had spread beyond the US to Japan. Deming was instrumental in popularising the quality control courses with emphasis on statistical methods. In 50's various new developments took place and new statistical quality control techniques were developed. Motivated by Deming's philosophy on quality control, K. Ishikawa the renowned Japanese quality control specialist began to implement Deming's concept with the objective of improving quality of Japanese products. Ishikawa introduced the control chart techniques in Japan (Banks, 1989). The European Organisation for quality control was formed which was evident of the interest taken by European countries in developing and disseminating knowledge of quality control. Hunter (1986) applied the exponentially weighted moving average (EWMA) in quality control.

A new phase dawned in the sixties. Feigenbaum (1983) described this era as total quality control which emphasised that quality control activity should not remain confined to the shop floor but it's scope should extend to analysing the results of statistical methods so that the decision making process is rational.

Total quality control advocated the idea that all departments, not only the quality control department, had quality control responsibilities. In 1960's itself such concepts as zero defects and Quality Circles came to the fore. To achieve the objective of zero defects worker motivation and involvement are essential pre-requisites. Similarly, in Quality Circles the supervisors and workers form group to meet frequently and address themselves to quality related problems. It results in education and training in quality control techniques, for all the quality circle group members. A number of magazines and journals began their publication in this period, prominent among them were Quality Progress, Journal of Quality Technology, and Quality. It was in the sixties itself that very foundation of consumerism movement was laid. Legal framework for product safety and reliability was developed and modified with the enactment of consumer product safety Act in 1967, Radiation Control for Health and Safety Act in 1968, and amendments to the U.S. Food, Drug and Cosmetic Act in 1969.

In 1970's Ishikawa broadened the concept of quality control to propagate the concept of 'company wide quality control' (Ishikawa, et al 1975). Feigenbaum (1983) referred to the same concept as 'total quality control organisation wide'. According to this approach, every worker right from the Chief Executive Officer to the machine operator was required to be involved in quality control. The significant point was that the top management must be actively involved in quality control. An all-embracing term 'quality system' came to be used to describe the collective plans, and activities to ensure that a product will satisfy given needs. Following definition of 'quality system' was given by Feigenbaum (1983) :

"The agreed on, company-wide and plant wide operating work structure, documented in effective, integrated technical and managerial procedures, for guiding the co-ordinated actions of the people, the machines, and the information of the company and plant in the best and most practical ways to assure customers quality satisfaction and economical costs of quality"

The concept of quality cost was given due attention in the 70's. In 1971, the American Society for Quality Control (ASQC) defined the various categories of quality costs. Wadsworth et al. (1986) classified these costs as preventive, appraisal, internal, and external. A major quality control development occurred in 1976. Ishikawa (1975) used cause-and-effect diagrams to solve quality problems. These diagrams were known as fish bone-plots or Ishikawa-diagrams. By mid 70's computers had come to be used in : automated testing, computer-aided-design (CAD), computer-aided-manufacturing (CAM), computer-aided-process control and in MIS. Computer-aided quality (CAQ) represents the totality of application of computer, to quality control. It could be operated from the same data base as CAD & CAM. The use of computers facilitated the application of advanced statistical quality control methods.

In 1980's, the emphasis of quality control shifted towards **quality management** and its human aspects. The abundance of application of statistical quality control techniques was another salient feature of this period. There are numerous statistical methods available for controlling quality levels of products. However there has been thrust on "management of quality system in recent times which attempt to control the quality levels of entire production process, thereby assuring a certain level of quality of out going products. Feigenbaum (1983) describes in detail the activities which are accountable to `quality management'. According to Kivenko (1984) the purpose of quality management is to manufacture a product whose quality is designed, produced, and maintained at the least possible cost, while meeting the contractual agreement with the customers.

CONCEPT OF QUALITY MANAGEMENT

Peters and Waterman (1982) pinpoint quality, in their famous book "In search of Excellence", as a characteristic prevalent in excellent corporations throughout the United States Mcdermott and Cound (1988) define quality as the sum of the attributes or properties that describe the product. These are generally expressed in terms of specific product characteristics such as dimensional, physical and chemical properties of the product. Macdonald & Piggot (1992) highlight the importance of quality management in contributing to customer satisfaction:

"What gives quality such importance is simply this : make goods or provide services which consistently delight the customers and your reputation will soar. Make goods which fall below customer expectation and almost without exception your customers will flock elsewhere. Much of Western industry today has a management problem - it is not competing efficiently in world markets - and it needs total quality management if it is to survive. There must be a total commitment to quality at every level of industry, beginning with top management."

The definition of quality as given in the Soviet Encyclopedia is "Quality of products, the aggregate of properties of a product determining its ability to satisfy the needs it was built to satisfy."

The European organisation for Quality Control Glossary (1981) gives the following definition for quality : "The totality of features and characteristics of a product or service that bear on its ability to satisfy a given need. N.B. with manufactured products quality is mainly determined by quality of design and quality of manufacture.

The word quality has multiple meanings. According to ANSI/ASQC (1983) standard A-3-1987 quality is "The totality of features and characteristics of a product or service that bear on its ability to satisfy stated or implied needs". Some other workers like Groocock (1980), Zaludova (1981), Thoday (1981), Groocock (1981) and Seghezzi (1981) have offered detailed views on the concept of quality and have tried to put to rest the debate that whether quality is conformance to standards or fitness for use.

Quality management has been referred by various terms such as quality assurance, quality function deployment, total quality control, Zero-defects and many more. Japan implemented it, after second world war, by the name company wide quality control. In CWQC it is emphasised that quality is every body's concern in the organisation. It also includes affiliated organisations like raw material suppliers, vendors and marketing intermediaries. Quality management encompasses these concepts and is relatively broader. Quality management is that aspect of the overall management function that determines and implement the quality policy.

Quality management practices relate to the operationalisation of quality policy and plans. The functions that all employees, right from top management to the worker's level, have to perform for achieving the set quality goals form quality management practices. This requires an attitudinal change which, then, has to percolate down the hierarchy to the workers level. The quality management practices are management-driven. Therefore, top management's vision and commitment for quality is a necessary prerequisite for adopting good quality management practices.

The concept of quality management embrace the whole organisation. Quality management recognizes the importance of broad systems issues and seeks effective ways of integrating the large number of people with large number of machines and huge quantities of information. Juran (1966) attributes 80% of all quality related faults to management. Mainly because the quality management covers the production cycle from product conception to customer service. The approach to securing quality is the subject of Quality Management. Currently world over this topic is discussed under the title of Total Quality Management (TQM) to cover its broader perspective. Total Quality Management is a way to continuously improve performance at every level of operation, in every functional area of an organisation, using all available human and capital resources. Quality management has become crucial to the survival of industry. The market in the 1980's was replete with special purpose software packages in quality control and quality assurance.

In 1990's the emphasis is being placed on activities like product design assurance, procurement quality assurance, production quality control, and product quality audits. Developments in these areas are of recent origin and are ongoing. These are essential parts of the total quality system. Development of international standards is another ongoing area of activity.

Following table lists the contributions of Pioneers in Quality Control

TABLE 1.1 Pioneers in Quality Control

Pioneer	Accomplishment
P.B. Crosby	Founded Quality College, Winter Park, Florida Initiated the quality cost reduction program "Buck a Day (BAD)" Developed the "14-Step Quality Improvement Program" Originated a widely used definition of quality Wrote Quality Is Free and numerous other popular books on quality Developed "Zero Defects", a 30-day quality program for a supervisor and 8 to 10 of the supervisor's employees
W.E. Deming	Developed quality control training during World War II Researched the use of statistics in quality control for the War Department during World War II Brought statistical methods in quality control to Japan after World War II Originated a definition of statistical quality control that emphasizes statistical aspects and economic goals of quality control Developed "14 points" (or obligations) of management's responsibility for quality and management of an enterprise Identified two separate causes ("special" and "common") for poor quality and responsibilities for their correction
H.F. Dodge	Founding member of the Western Electric Inspection Department (the department de-

	veloped theories and methods of quality control and quality assurance) Developed basic concepts of sampling inspection by attributes Defined consumer's risks and producer's risks Member of a group of statisticians and engineers formed by the War Department to conduct research in the use of statistics in quality control (the group developed standard inspection procedures and sampling tables) Initiated widespread applications of control chart techniques throughout Western Electric Prepared the ASTM manual on presentation of data Chairman of ASA Committee Z1 Developed the Dodge-Romig Sampling Inspection Tables on attribute acceptance sampling Developed first continuous sampling plans Developed skip-lot sampling plans Developed chain sampling plans
G.D. Edwards	Founding member of the Western Electric Inspection Department Taught courses on the use of statistical quality control throughout manufacturing plants in the United States during World War II
A.V. Feigenbaum	Developed the concept of total quality control Identified five stages in the history and evolution of quality control
R.A. Freund	Member of the ASQC committee for precision in terminology which prepared "Definitions, Symbols, Formulas and Tables for Control Charts" Developed an acceptance control chart for sample or subgroup variability
F.E. Grubbs	Developed tables for attributes sampling plans
F.M. Gryna	Developed, together with Juran, the concept of operator self-control (by this concept, control must be delegated to the operator in the workplace)

H. Hotelling	Member of the Statistical Research Group at Columbia University during World War II (the group developed sequential analysis, and multivariate analysis in quality control) Developed the t^2 statistic
K. Ishikawa	Introduced control chart methods to Japan Developed cause-and-effect diagram Acclaimed as the "father of quality circles" Suggested intervals in construction of histograms used in quality control Indicated the use of paired barplots in quality control
J.M. Juran	Renowned international consultant in quality control Member of a group of engineers that assisted the Western Electric Inspection Department Developed many concepts in quality (his workis creadited as being the basis of Japan's postwar management) Developed one of the general definitions of quality Espoused the application of the Pareto principle in quality control Developed the alternative designations sporadic and chronic for the causes of poor quality Developed, in conjunction with Gryna, the concept of operator self control
E. Pearson	Developed British standards on the application of statistical methods to industrial standardization and quality control Developed estimation curves Indicated the use of range and its properties in quality control
D.A. Quarles	Founding member of the Western Electric Inspection Department
H.G. Romig	Developed, along with Dodge, the Dodge-Romig Sampling Inspection Tables on attributes acceptance sampling
J. Scanlon	Developed the Scanlon Plan for employee motivation

W.A. Shewhart	Founding member of the Western Electric Inspection Department Developed the first control charts Formed one of the groups sponsored by the War Department during World War II to conduct research on the use of statistics in quality control Developed the concept of assignable causes Developed basic concepts of type I and type II error
G. Taguchi	Development methods for quality improvement studies using experimental design procedures (explored the concept of off-line quality control)
M.N. Torrey	Later member of the Western Electric Inspection Department Further developed CSP, in conjunction with Dodge
A. Wald	Member of the Statistical Research Group at Columbia University during World War II Developed sequential-sampling plans, procedures and tables Proposed truncation value in sequential sampling plans Developed general expression for average sample numbers (ASN) Developed parametric equations for OC curves for sequential sampling plan

Source : Banks, J., 1989. *Principles of Quality Control*, New York: John Wiley & Sons, pp. 24 - 26.

ISO-9000 SERIES AND QUALITY MANAGEMENT

Standardisation plays a vital role in management of technology. It is the process of consolidating the knowledge and experience at any given time and documenting the same for wide application. The standards operate at the industry, association, national and international level. The International Standards Organisation (ISO) first published ISO-9000 series of standards in 1987. It is an international set of documents written by members of a world wide delegation known as the ISO/Technical Committee 176. The ISO/TC 176 consists of three standard committees and several working groups. Five national associations participate in the ISO/TC 176 as convenors of subcommittees, they are : AFNOR (Association Francaise deNormalisation), ANSI (American National Standards Institute), BSI (British Standards Institute), NNI (Netherlands Normalisation Institute), and SCC (Standards Council of Canada). Other member countries are also represented by their respective national bodies. India is represented by BIS (Bureau of Indian Standards). Lamprecht (1992) gives in the tabular form national standards equivalent to the ISO-9000 series.

In the above table the Indian equivalent to ISO-9000 series is given as IS 10201 series. While Indian standard on Quality Management and Quality System Elements guidelines (1992) refer to the same as IS-14000 series. These are listed below :

International Standard	Corresponding Indian Standard	Degree of Equivalence
ISO 8402 : 1986	IS 13999 : 1988 Quality systems - Vocabulary	Identical
ISO 9000 : 1987	IS 14000 : 1989 Quality systems - Guidelines for selection & use of standards on quality systems	Identical
ISO 9001 : 1987	IS 14001 : 1989 Quality systems - Model for quality assurance in design/development, production, installation and servicing	Identical
ISO 9002 : 1987	IS 14002 : 1989 Quality systems - Model for quality assurance in production and installation	Identical
ISO 9002 : 1987	IS 14003 : 1989 Quality systems - Model for quality assurance in final inspection and test	Identical
ISO 9004 : 1987	IS 14004 : 1991 Quality Management and quality system elements - Guidelines--	Identical

Table 1.2 National Standards Equivalent to the ISO 9000 Series

Standards Body	Quality Management & quality assurance standards: Guidelines for selection and use	Quality Systems: model for QA in design/dvp. production, installation and servicing	Quality Systems: model for QA in production and installation	Quality Systems: model for QA in final inspection and test	Quality Mngt. and quality systems guidelines
ISO	ISO 9000:87	ISO 9001:87	ISO 9002:87	ISO 9003:87	ISO 9004:87
Australia	AS 3900	AS 3901	AS 3902	AS 3903	AS 3904
Austria	OE NORM-PREN 29000	OE NORM-PREN 29001	OE NORM-PREN 29002	OE NORM-PREN 29003	OE NORM-PREN 29004
Belgium	NBNX 50-0020-1	NBN X 50-003	NBN X 50-004	NBN X 50-005	NBN X 50-002-2
Canada	-	-	-	-	CSA Q420-87
China	GB/T 10300.1-88	GB/T 10300.2-88	GB/T 100300.3-88	GB/T 10300.4-88	GB/T 10300.5-88
Denmark	DS/EN 29000	DS/EN 29001	DS/EN 29002	DS/EN 29003	DS/EN 29004
European	EN 29000:87	EN 29001:87	EN 29002:87	EN 29003:87	EN 29004:87
Finland	SFS-ISO 9000	SFS-ISO 9001	SFS-ISO 9002	SFS-ISO 9003	SFS-ISO 9004
France	NF X 50-121	NF X 50-131	NF X 50-132	NF X 50-133	NF X 50-122
Hungary	MI 18990-88	MI 18991-88	MI 18992-88	MI 18993-88	MI 18994-88
India	IS:10201 Part 2	IS:10201 Part 4	IS:10201 Part 5	IS:10201 Part 6	IS:10201 Part 3

Ireland	IS 300 Part 0	IS 300 Part 1	IS 300 Part 2	IS 300 Part 3	IS 300 Part 0
Italy	UNI/EN 29000-1987	UNI/EN 29001-1987	UNI/EN 29002-1987	UNI/EN 29003-1987	UNI/EN 29004-1987
Malaysia	-	MS 985/ISO 9001:87	MS 985/ISO 9002:87	MS 985/ISO 9003:87	-
Netherlands	NEN-ISO 9000	NEN-ISO 9001	NEN-ISO 9002	NEN-ISO 9003	NEN-ISO 9004
New Zealand	NZS 5600: Part 1	NZS 5601-87	NZS 5602-87	NZS 5603-87	NZS 5600: Part 2-1987
Norway	NS-EN 29000	NS-EN 29001	NS-ISO 9002	NS-ISO 9003	-
South Africa	SABS 0157: Part0	SABS 0157: Part I	SABS 0157: Part II	SABS 0157: Part III	SABS 0157: Part IV
Spain	UNE 66 900	UNE 66 901	UNE 66 902	UNE 66 903	UNE 66 904
Sweden	SS-ISO 9000	SS-ISO 9001	SS-ISO 9002	SS-ISO 9003	SS-ISO 9004
Switzerland	SN-ISO 9000	SN-ISO 9001	SN-ISO 9002	SN-ISO 9003	SN-ISO 9004
Tunisia	NT 110.18	NT 110.19	NT 110.20	NT 110.21	NT 110.22
U. Kingdom	BS 5750: Part 0 Section 0.1	BS 5750: PArt 1	BS 5750: Part 2	BS 5750: Part 3	BS 5750: Part 4
USA	ANSI/ASQC Q90	ANSI/ASQC Q91	ANSI/ASQC Q92	ANSI/ASQC Q93	ANSI/ASQC Q94
USSR	-	40.9001-87	40.9002-87	-	-
Germany	DIN ISO 9000	DIN ISO 9001	DIN ISO 9002	DIN ISO 9003	DIN ISO 9004
Yugoslavia	JUS A.K. 1.010	JUS A.K. 1.012	JUS A.K. 1.013	JUS A.K. 1.014	JUS A.K. 1.011

Source : Lamprecht, J.L., 1992. ISO 9000 : Preparing For Registration, New York : Marcel Dekkar Inc.,

ISO - 9000 SERIES

The ISO-9000 series of standards act as bench mark against which an organisation can compare its own quality management practices. These standards are generic in nature and are applicable to the quality management system of all types of organisation. The ISO-9000 series consists of five documents which are models of quality assurance namely ISO 9001, ISO 9002 and ISO 9003. The three model, for quality assurance represent three district forms of functional or organizational capability suitable for two party contractual purposes. The ISO 9000 and ISO 9004 are supporting guidelines documents. The ISO 9000 set of guidelines help potential users (both customers/purchasers and suppliers) decide which quality assurance model (viz ISO 9001, 9002, and 9003) is most appropriate and relevant to a contractual relationship. The ISO 9004 provide guidelines for developing and implementing quality management system. Therefore ISO 9000 and ISO 9004 series of documents should not be treated as the models of quality assurance and they should not be perceived as sets of mandatory requirements. Registration can be obtained for any one of the quality assurance models, viz ISO 9001, ISO 9002, and ISO 9003. The focus of these standards is on documenting the operational techniques and managerial activities used to fulfill customer expectations and requirements. These models were not written for any specific industry. However some industries have issued their own set of interpretive guidelines. For example U.K.'s Chemical Industries Association has issued ISO 9001 EN 29001 'Guidelines for use by the Chemical and Allied Industries.' These guidelines provide little additional information. The international committee has organised the ISO quality assurance documents in to three broad categories viz ISO 9001, 9002, and 9003 on the basis of contractual obligations for customer supplier relationships. (Lamprecht, 1992) ISO 9001 is applicable in contractual situations when "conformance to specified requirements is to be assured during several stages which may include design/development, production, installation, and servicing." Moreover,

a) The contract requires design effort and the product requirements are stated principally in performance terms or they need to be established;
b) Confidence in product conformance can be attained by adequate demonstration of certain supplier's capabilities in design, development, production, installation, and servicing.

ISO 9002, the standard often adopted (in the U.S. and abroad) by the chemical and process industries, as well as other industries, is applicable in contractual situations when :

a) The specific requirements for the product are stated in terms of an established design or specification;
b) Confidence in product conformance can be attained by adequate demonstration of a certain supplier's capabilities in production and installation.

ISO 9003, which has been applied to small shops, distributors or divisions within an organization, is applicable in contractual situations when :

The conformance of the product to specified requirements can be shown with adequate confidence providing that certain supplier's capabilities for inspection and tests .mb7

conducted on the product supplied can be satisfactorily demonstrated on completion.

This partitioning along contractual obligations is both logical and practical. For instance, whereas ISO 9003 suppliers only have to demonstrate, among other things, a capability to inspect and test a product (e.g., using proper acceptance sampling plans, monitoring test equipments, etc.). ISO 9002 suppliers are expected to go further and demonstrate that the relevant manufacturing processes are capable of maintaining requirements as per design specifications (e.g., perform machine and/or process capability studies). ISO 9001 suppliers have to go further yet, and must also demonstrate a capability/mastering in all phases of design, development and servicing.

The table given below mentions the cross reference list of Quality System Elements.

Table 1.3 Cross-References List of Quality System Elements

Title	Corresponding Paragraph (or subsection) Nos. in		
	9001	**9002**	**900**
Management Responsibility	4.1	4.1a	4.1b
Quality System Principles	4.2	4.2	4.2a
Contract Review	4.3	4.3	-
Design Control	4.4	-	-
Document Control	4.5	4.4	4.3a
Purchasing	4.6	4.5	-
Purchaser Supplier Product	4.7	4.6	-
Product Identification and Traceability	4.8	4.7	4.5a
Control of Production	4.9	4.8	-
Inspection and Testing	4.10	4.9	4.5a
Inspection, Measuring and Test Equip.	4.11	4.10	4.6a
Inspection and Test Status	4.12	4.11	4.7a
Control of Nonconforming Product	4.13	4.12	4.8a
Corrective Action	4.14	4.13	-
Handling, Storage, Packaging and Delivery	4.15	4.14	4.9a
Quality Records	4.16	4.15	4.10a
Internal Audits	4.17	4.16a	-
Training	4.18	4.17a	4.1b
After-sales Servicing	4.19	-	-
Statistical Techniques	4.20	4.18	4.12a

a Less stringent than 9001 **b** Less stringent than 9002
- Element not present
Unmarked paragraphs indicate Full Requirement
Source : Lamprecht, J.L., 1992. *ISO 9000 : Preparing for Registration,* Newyork, Marcel Dekker Inc., p 7.

ISO 9001 quality assurance model is the most stringent model with all the 20 quality system elements applicable, while ISO 9002 comes next with 18 quality system elements and ISO 9003 is the least stringent with only 12 quality system elements Sections on Design-Control and after sales servicing are not included in the ISO 9002 model. ISO 9003 quality assurance model does not include following eight quality system elements : Contract Review, Design control, Purchasing, Purchaser supplied product, Control of production, Corrective action, Internal audits and After sales servicing.

More than eighty five percent of organisations registered to one of the quality assurance models, choose either ISO 9001 and ISO 9002 (Lamprecht, 1992). If an organisation is involved with design and development activities then it should go for ISO 9001 otherwise registration to ISO 9002 is sufficient.

More and more organisations are vying for registration to one of the three quality assurance models. Customers request their suppliers to seek accreditation to one of the ISO 9000 series of standards and the suppliers, in turn request their suppliers and so on down the line. This is termed as the 'cascading effect'. The ISO 9000 series of standards should not be referred to as a set of 'specifications' (product or otherwise) it does not affect or complement product specification but it is an standard for the implementation and management of a quality assurance system. It is not a technical document but a generic document intended to apply to all industries.

Another myth about the ISO 9000 series is that it is to be used by European Community as trade barrier for all types of product categories with effect from 1st January 1993. Infact European Community issued product liability directive in July 1985 and product safety directive in July 1989, which requires the implementation of a quality system (hence the need for an ISO 9000 type quality assurance system). This directive covers following industries :

(i) Building products
(ii) Gas appliances
(iii) Lifting and loading equipment
(iv) Machine safety
(v) Medical devices
(vi) Mobile machines
(vii) Personal protection equipment

(viii) Radio interference
(ix) Rollover protection
(x) Simple pressure vessels
(xi) Small industrial trucks
(xii) Telecommunication terminal equipment, and
(xiii) Toys

STEPS IN ISO 9000 CERTIFICATION

Gupta (1994) gives the following five steps which are involved in ISO 9000 registration :

(i) Select the appropriate standards using guidelines given in ISO 9000.
(ii) Prepare quality manual to cover all the elements of the selected quality assurance model using guidelines given in ISO 9004.
(iii) Develop & document proper procedures and shop floor instructions which may be necessary for implementation of the quality system.
(iv) Conduct self audit to check compliance of selected model.
(v) Select a registrar and apply for certification and registration.

QMI'S 10 STEPS FOR REGISTRATION

UK based Quality Management International (QMI) is a leading organisation in quality management and is dedicated to setting new standards and transforming company cultures. QMI offers following ten steps plan for registration to ISO 9000.

(1) Set up a steering group.
(2) Develop Strategic Plan, Vision, Mission & Goals.
(3) Review current status relative to ISO 9001, 2 or 3.
(4) Establish a training plan.
(5) Develop Quality Policy Manual & Procedures Manual.
(6) Develop Internal Audit Capability.
(7) Meet with Assessment body.

(8) Submit manual for approval.
(9) Assessment visit.
(10) Registration.

FUTURE PLANS OF ISO

The International Standards Organisation is revising some of its existing ISO-9000 series of standards and coming out with some new standards. With this,anomalies such as absence of standards for services and software would be checked. The table gives the complete listing of existing and new standards and also the standards for which work is in progress :

Table 1.4 : ISO 9000 Standards

Existing Standards	
ISO 9000	Quality Management and Quality Assurance Standards - Guidelines for Selection and Use
ISO 9001	Quality System - Model for Quality Assurance in Design/Development, Production, Installation and Servicing
ISO 9002	Quality System - Model for Quality Assurance in Production and Installation
ISO 9003	Quality Systems - Model for Quality Assurance in Final Inspection and Test
ISO 9004	Quality Management and Quality System Elements-Guidelines
ISO 8402	Quality Management and Quality Assurance- Vocabulary .
New Standards	
ISO 9004-2	Quality Management and Quality System Element-Part 2 : Guidelines for Services
ISO 9000-3	Quality Management and Quality Assurance Standards - Part 3 : Guidelines for the Application of ISO 9001 to the Development, supply, and Maintenance of software
ISO 10011-1	Guidelines for Auditing Quality Systems-Part 1: Auditing
ISO 10011-2	Guidelines for Auditing Quality Systems-Part 2: Qualification Criteria for Quality System Auditors
ISO 10011-3	Guidelines for Auditing Quality Systems-part 3: Managing Audit programs
ISO 10012-1	Quality Assurance Requirements for Measuring Equipment-Part 1: Metrological Confirmation System for Measuring Equipment

Works in Progress

ISO 9000-1	**Revision to ISO 9000**
ISO 9000-2	**Quality Management and Quality Systems Elements-Part 2: Guidelines for Implementing ISO 9001, ISO 9002, and ISO 9003. ISO 9000-4 Quality Management and Quality Assurance Standards-Part 4: Application for Dependability Management ISO 9004-1 Revision of ISO 9004**
ISO 9004-3	**Quality Management and Quality Systems Elements-Part 3: Guidelines for Processed Materials**
ISO 9004-4	**Quality Management and Quality Systems Elements-Part 4: Guidelines for Quality Improvement**
ISO 9005-1	**Quality Management and Quality Systems Elements-Part 5: Guidelines for Quality Plans**
ISO 9006-6	**Quality Management and Quality Systems Elements-Part 6: Guidelines for Configuration Management**
ISO 10012-2	**Quality Assurance Requirements for Measuring Equipment-Part 2: Measurement Assurance**

Unnumbered Guidelines Document on Project Management
Note : Numbering for works in progress can change.
Source : Gupta, H.D., 1994. Quality Assurance through ISO 9000, Delhi : South Asia Publications.

ISO 9000 & QUALITY MANAGEMENT PRACTICES

Total quality management (TQM) is a company wide strategic approach to improve the quality of products and services through continuous improvement of it's operations. For seeking ISO 9000 registration, greater emphasis is placed on documenting the procedure of quality assurance. This documented procedure serves as the guidelines for implementing the total quality system. It also acts as the yard stick for auditors/assessors to assess the extent to which the documented procedure is adopted, while meeting the contractual agreement with the customers. It embraces design, manufacturing, marketing of a product and other functional areas such as personnel, finance, training, public relations, etc. Total Quality Management is not synonymous with ISO 9000 or other quality system standards. There are some companies with ISO 9000 certification which do not practice total quality management. Similarly some total quality companies do not find it necessary to obtain ISO 9000 registration.

PROGRESS IN INDIA

In India the largest single organisation at the national level is Bureau of Indian Standards (BIS). BIS establishes national standards and has prepared over 16000 standards in various disciplines (Parmeshvar, 1993). The ISO 9000 series of standards are recognised in India by BIS which has issued its identical equivalent standards. A large number of Indian Business Organisations are preparing themselves to systematically introduce quality management practices to comply with one of these standards. (Singh, 1992) The ISO 9000 certification enhances image and prestige of the organisation in world market. It is considered as reliability stamp to prove that the organisation follows world class quality system practices.

A seminar was held on "ISO 9000 Challenges to the Textile Industry" on 12th June 1993 in Surat. It was organised by Textile Committee, Bombay. Aspects like elements of quality system, implementation strategy, importance of documentation in ISO 9000, experience sharing, implication of ISO 9000 in textile units, etc were discussed in the day long seminar (Gandhi 1993).

In India there are 102 companies which are already certified as meeting the ISO 9000 requirements (Singh, 1993). In contrast a small company like U.K. is having 14000 companies with ISO 9000 registration (Gandhi, 1992). At present there are nearly 180 companies in India which meet the ISO 9000 requirements. The manufacturing organisations are predominant in getting registration to the ISO 9000 series of standards. Most of the organisations have selected either ISO 9001 or 9002 as the model for quality assurance which is in agreement with findings of Lamprecht (1992).

ORGANISATION FOR QUALITY MANAGEMENT

Organisation is one of the most important element of management in any field of human activity. Organisation makes use of specialisation by allocating its specific jobs to those persons who are considered most suitable for those jobs. The type of organisational structure varies with the nature of activity to be managed. The objective of organising is to facilitate effective management. Lal (1990) classified quality function into two distinct groups, namely **Quality Engineering & Quality Control**. Quality Engineering mainly deals with developing, defining and planning of quality during the pre-production stage. Quality control is concerned with improving and implementing quality plans during the in-process and post-production stages. Lal (1990) describes the detailed work elements for both Quality Engineering and Quality Control.

Quality Engineering

This comprises of specialist staff functions as well as activities connected with the development, defining, and planning of quality during the pre-production stage. Its main work elements are given below :

(a) Advice to the Management on the quality policy of the company and laying down realistic quality objectives.

(b) The analysis of the customers quality requirements and the formulation of design specifications.

(c) The review and evaluation of product design with a view to improving quality and reducing quality costs.

(d) Defining quality standards and preparation of product specifications.

(e) Planning process controls and formulation of procedures to ensure quality conformance.

(f) Development of quality control techniques and inspection methods including the design of special test equipment.

(g) Conducting process-capability studies.

(h) Analysis of quality costs.

(i) Planning and Organising quality control for incoming stores and materials including the capacity verification of the vendors.

(j) Quality audit of the company.
(k) Organising training in quality programme.

Quality Control

It is concerned with the interpretation and implementation of quality plans. It comprises of inprocess and postproduction testing, which are aimed at ensuring the quality conformance of products. The main work elements are enumerated below :

(a) Assistance in establishing quality controls at various points of the manufacturing process.
(b) Maintenance and calibration of process control equipment.
(c) Investigation of defects and assistance in solving quality problems during production.
(d) Implementation of quality control measures for incoming materials and stores.
(e) Running a test laboratory for carrying out necessary test and analysis.
(f) Organising stage or interstage inspection or spot checks whenever required.
(g) Arranging final inspection to assess the quality of the end-product and the effectiveness of quality control measures.
(h) Checking the quality of the packaging to ensure that the product is able to withstand transportation hazards.
(i) Conducting tests for the measurement and analysis of goods on which customer complaints have been received.
(j) Feedback of defect data and customer complaints to the Quality Engineering Section.

It is not necessary that all the work elements will have to be performed by quality department personnel. To ensure effective quality management, these tasks must be performed by the most appropriate individuals or group/s.

However, the decentralisation of quality function should be attempted cautiously so that substantial number of defective products are not produced, due to the relatively larger feed back loop. It is observed, especially in complex high-speed production lines. Quality function is generally decentralised in those organisations where established quality control programmes are in force. Quality management is essentially an advisory function and therefore it is a staff function. The main task is to advise and assist other departments in attaining quality objectives. The internal structure of the quality department is generally a line organisation, because quality is it's prime function.

Main responsibilities of quality department are : inspection, testing, planning, quality engineering, quality training, and quality auditing. Groocock (1974) gives the following typical organisational structure, in which variations are possible :

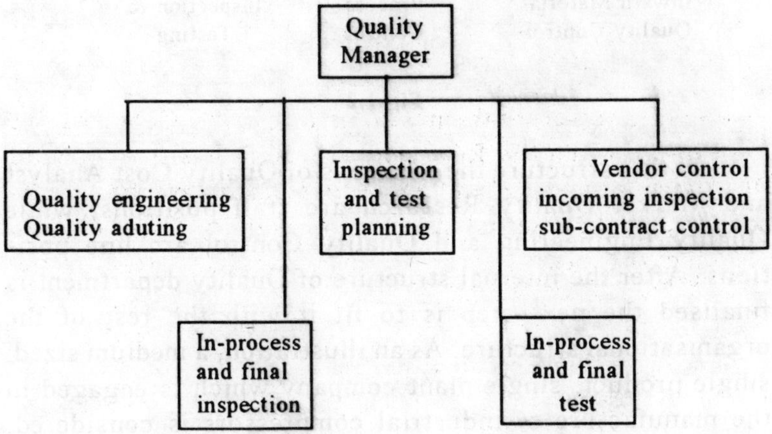

Fig. 1.1
(Example of quality department organisation)

In many organisations inspection and testing group report to the manufacturing department. Inspection and testing group should however report to the quality department, so that it is free from the pressures of the group whose quality they have to measure.

Lal (1990) offers a variation of the above organisational structure of the quality department.

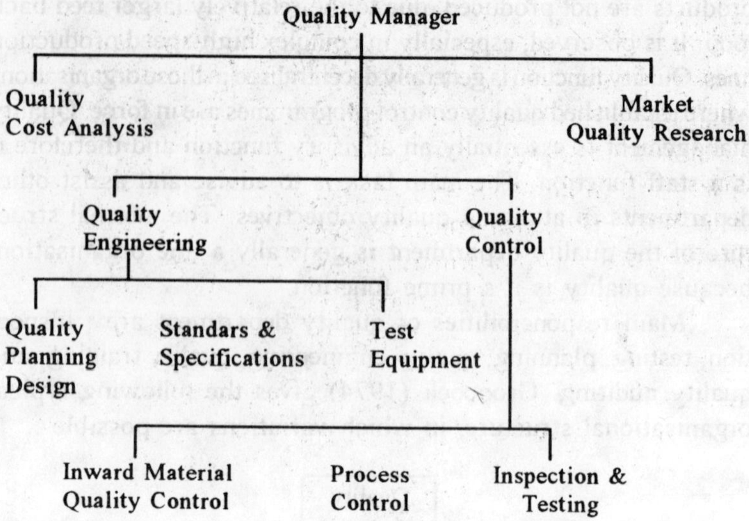

Fig 1.2

In this structure the positions of Quality Cost Analyst and Market Quality Research are staff positions, while Quality Engineering and Quality Control are line positions. After the internal structure of Quality department is finalised the next step is to fit it with the rest of the organisational structure. As an illustration, a medium sized, single product, single plant company which is engaged in the manufacture of industrial compressors is considered. It's organisational structure is given below with emphasis on quality department :

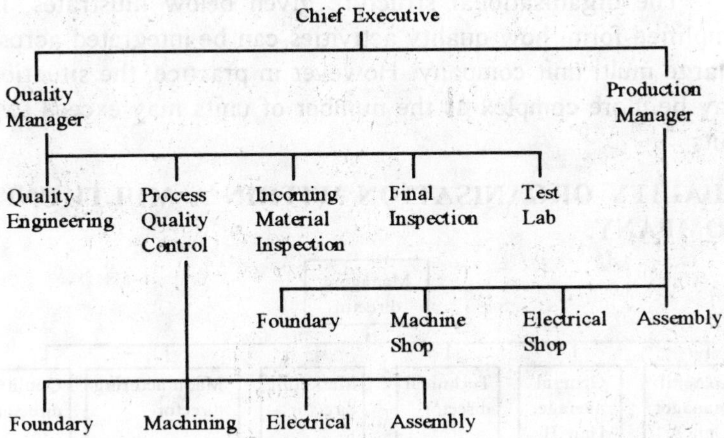

Fig 1.3

In the above structure, the quality manager is also responsible for Raw Material inspection, final inspection and managing the activities of test laboratory in addition to the functions of quality engineering and quality control. The activity of quality control is further, subdivided in to work station wise inspection groups. One significant point of the above structure is that both quality manager and production manager are reporting at the same level to the Chief Executive Officer. In some organisations the quality manager is made to report to the production manager which is not appropriate. It may be the case in small-sized organisations where the levels of hierarchy may be less. Groocock (1974) strongly recommends that the quality manager should not be at the same reporting level as the production superintendent, the industrial engineer, the production control manager etc. All of them report to the production manager. According to Groocock (1974) the practice of quality manager reporting to the production manager is wrong, as one of the responsibility of the quality department is to conduct quality audit of the work of other departments including manufacturing.

The organisational structure given below illustrates, in simplified form, how quality activities can be integrated across a large multi unit company. However in practice, the situation may be more complex as the number of units may exceed two units.

QUALITY ORGANISATION WITHIN A MULTI UNIT COMPANY.

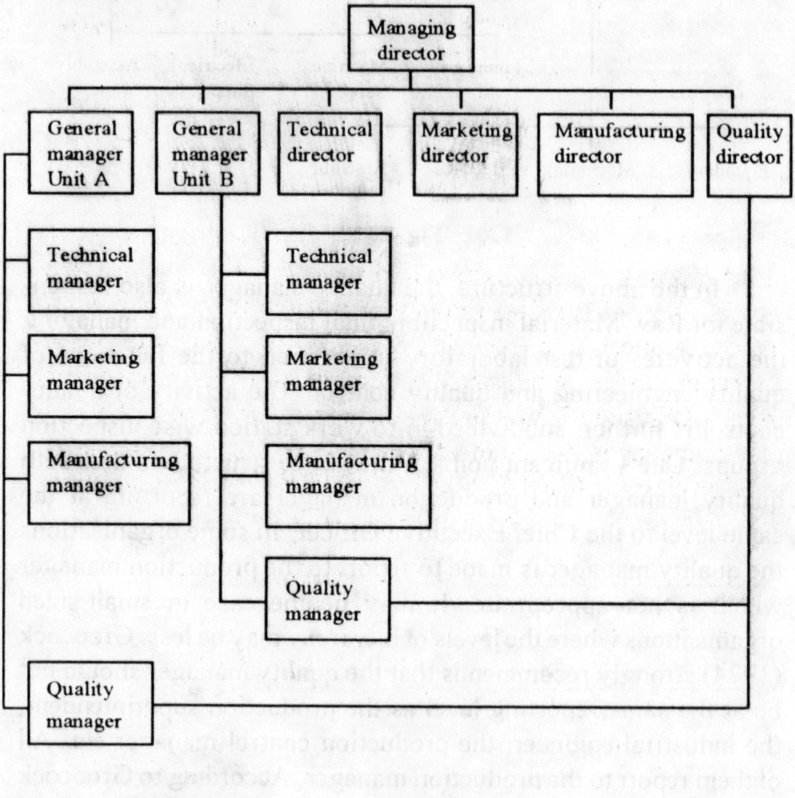

Fig 1.4

Source : Groocock, J.M., 1974. The Cost of Quality, London, Pitman Publishing, p. 45.

In the above structure unitwise quality managers report to the top management through their respective unit General Managers. The line position of quality managers have a functional responsibility to the quality director, a staff position. The major task of the quality director is to provide leadership to the quality function throughout the company as a whole.

In a multi plant organisation where the products are manufactured at many plants located at various geographical situations distant from the company headquarter, it may not be practical to have a comprehensive unit quality manager. But in such a situation the plant quality managers, one for each plant, should be appointed.

QUALITY MANAGEMENT : SCENARIO IN MADHYA PRADESH

Madhya Pradesh is one of the industrially backward states of our country, despite having abundance of natural resources and peaceful industrial climate. Madhya Pradesh is a state with the largest area in the country and unlimited possibilities for industrialisation exist. MP ranks second in the country in mineral wealth, second in the production of oilseeds, and third in food production. The first optical fibre unit in the country is situated in Madhya Pradesh. Giant sized industrial organisations like Bhilai Steel Plant, Bharat Heavy Electricals Ltd and Nepa mills are pride of MP.

A Dry port has been established in Pithampur near Indore. It will give a fillip to exports from this area. On the similar lines, Container Corporation of India is planning to open up container depots in Gwalior and Raipur also. It will facilitate transportation system for exports. Immense potential for improvement exists, if the maintenance of good quality of products is given the top priority. After the economic liberalisation policies of the government industrial development in Madhya Pradesh has accelerated, which is evident from the fact that nearly Rs. 30,836 crores have been invested in various projects in the state. It is 10.41% of the national total of Rs. 2,96,167 crores. It resulted in an increase of 8.48% in the rate of employment in the state. Madhya Pradesh ranks among the top four investment destinations in the country along with Maharashtra, Gujrat and Uttarpradesh. Investments over Rs. 25000 crores are already under implementation in flourishing growth centers like Pithampur and Dewas near Indore, Siltara and Urla near Raipur, Malanpur near Gwalior and Mandideep near Bhopal. In fact 125 new large and medium sector units have come up in just the last three years. Madhya Pradesh's industrial policy reflects government's 'industrialist/entrepreneur friendly' attitude. Salient features of the new industrial policy of Madhya Pradesh are :

* Single - window functioning at growth centers.
* Allotment of land on 99-year lease.
* Encourage private sector participation in power generation and infrastructure development.
* Attractive tax exemptions and deferred payments.
* Concept of 'No Industry Blocks', having extraordinary exemptions and deferments.
* Special facilities to encourage 100% EOUs.
* Scope of the 'Thrust Sector' enlarged.

Gradually, industrial organisations of M.P. are becoming quality conscious and some of them are even vying for ISO-9000 accredition. At present three industrial organisations of Madhya Pradesh have been awarded the coveted ISO-9000 certification. They are, Bhilai Steel Plant, Bharat Heavy Electricals Ltd and Kirloskar Brothers Ltd. It is testimony to the fact that these organisations have world class quality management practices in place. ISO 9000 accredition is a reliability stamp for value chain (production) process (rather than the product itself) right from the design stage through manufacturing, delivery, installation to the after sales service stages.

REFERENCES

American Society for Quality Control, Statistics Division, 1983. Glossary and Tables for Statistical Quality Control, 2nd ed., Milwaukee, Wis.

Banks, Jerry, 1989. Principles of Quality Control, New York, Johnwiley and Sons.

Bureau of Indian Standards, 1992. Quality Management And Quality System Elements - Guidelines, Third Revision, New Delhi.

Dodge, H.F. and Romig, H.G., 1941. "Single Sampling and Double Sampling Inspection Tables". As Quated in Banks (1989), Op. Cit.

Dodge, H.F. and Romig, H.G. 1944. Sampling Inspection Tables. As Quoted by Banks (1998), Op. Cit.

"Egypt", The Encyclopedia Americana, 1985. Vol. 10, Danbury, pp. 1 - 64.

European Organisation for Quality Control, 1981. Glossary of Terms Used in Quality Control, 5th Ed., Berne, Switzerland.

Feigenbaum, A.V., 1983. Total Quality Control. New York : McGraw Hill.

Gandhi, R.S., 1993. "ISO-9000-Challenges to the Textile Industry". New Cloth Market, Aug., pp. 8 - 10.

Groocock, J.M., 1974. The Cost of Quality, London, Pitman Publishing, pp. 30 - 45.

Groocock, J.M., 1980. "Conformance or Fitness for Use ? EOQC Quality, Vol. 2, pp. 3 - 6.

Groocock, J.M., 1981. "Conformance or Fitness for use ? (II)". EOQC Quality, Vol. 4, pp. 5 - 7.

Gupta, H.D., 1994. Quality Assurance Through ISO-9000, Delhi, South Asia Publications.

Hunter, J.S., 1986. "The Exponentially Weighted Moving Average". Journal of Quality Technology. Vol. 18, No. 4, pp. 203 - 210.

Ishikawa, K., et.al. 1975. "Quality Control Activities of Foreign Countries Through Japanese Eyes". As Quoted by Banks (1989), Op. Cit.

Jennett, W.J. and Welch, D.L., 1939. "The Control of Proportion Defective as Judged by a single Quality Characteristic Varying on a continuous Scale". As Quoted by Banks (1989), OP. Cit.

Juran, J.M., 1966. "Quality Problems, Remedies and Nostrums". Industrial Quality Control, Vol. 22, No. 12, pp. 647 - 653.

Kivenko, K., 1984. Quoted in Banks, J., 1989. Op.Cit. p. 30.

Lal, H., 1990. Total Quality Management - A Practical Approach, New Delhi, Wiley-Eastern Ltd., pp. 39 - 50.

Lamprecht, J.L. 1992. ISO 9000 : Preparing For Registration. New York : Marcel Dekker Inc. .lh7

Macdonald, J. and Piggott, J., 1992. Global Quality The New Management Culture, New Delhi : Viva Books Pvt. Ltd..

McDermott, T.C. and Cound, D.M., 1988. "Inspection and Quality Control". In Ireson, W.G. and Grant, E.L. (Eds.) Handbook of Industrial Engineering and Management, New Delhi: Prentice Hall India, pp. 703 - 751.

Paramesvar, K.R., 1993. ''Role of Standards in Technology Management'' Productivity, Vol. 33, No. 4, Jan-March, pp. 596 - 600.

Peters, T.J. and Waterman, R.H., 1982. In Search of Excellence - Lessons from America's Best Run Companies, New York, Harper and Row, Publishers.

Seghezzi, H.D., 1981. ''What is Quality ? Conformance with Requirements or Fitness for the Intended Use ?''. EOQC Quality, Vol. 4, pp. 3 - 4.

Singh, A., 1992. ''ISO 9000 : An Opportunity or a Nightmare''. Productivity, Vol. 33, No. 1, April-June, pp. 110 - 113.

Singh, A. 1993. ''Quality & the Competitive Environment''. Productivity, Vol. 34, No.3, October-December, pp. 431 - 436.

Thoday, W.R., 1981. Additional Reflections on Quality Terminology''. EOQC Quality, Vol.1, p. 11.

Wadsworth, H.M., Stephens, K.S. and Godfrey, A.B., 1986. Modern Methods for Quality Control and Improvement, New york, Wiley.

Zaludova, A.H., 1981. ''Some Reflections on Quality Terminology''. EOQC Quality, Vol. 1, pp. 3 - 10. .lh8

CHAPTER 2

STUDIES IN QUALITY MANAGEMENT : A REVIEW

The subject area of Quality Management is abundant with rich information. Both academicians and practioners alike have contributed to the literature. Since the subject is of recent origin, there are some 'living legends', who are termed as 'Quality Gurus', they continue to propound newer concepts and theories. There is fast growing literature on various aspects of Quality Management. The review of literature is focussed on those books, research papers, articles and studies that address quality from an organisation-wide managerial point of view.

In this chapter, literature relevant to the following aspects of Quality Management has been reviewed, viz. :

Contributions of Quality Gurus and Factors of Quality Management, Quality Management Practices, Quality and Productivity and Indian studies in the area of Quality Management. A number of books, handbooks, journals, magazines and newspapers have been surveyed.

FACTORS OF QUALITY MANAGEMENT

Three American experts on quality namely Philip Crosby, W.E. Deming and J.M. Juran have contributed immensely to the fast growing literature on Quality Management and Practices thereof. Their contributions are so important that they have been referred in the literature as 'Quality Gurus'. Many consultants offer solutions to the problems of achieving quality improvements based on the teachings of these Quality Gurus.

Feigenbaum has pioneered in the area of Total Quality Control aspects. Japanese have relied heavily in the past on teachings of Deming and Juran. Now, Japan has their own experts on Quality namely K. Ishikawa, G. Taguchi and M.Imai.

Jeremy Main (1986) addressed the question "which Guru should your company choose?" and continues further, 'The menu of possibilities is widely varied, with offerings that range from the bland to the incendiary. Do you want an inspirational type like Phil Crosby, who will send the corporate staff charging up the hill under a banner inscribed Zero Defects? Or do you want a technical type...who will work quietly alongside your engineers? Perhaps you masochistically crave fiery denunciations from the 85-year-old W. Edwards Deming, who will probably tell your managers they are a pack of idiots.'

On the same issue Macdonald & Piggot (1992) believe that no one expert can have monopoly of all wisdom on the subject of quality. 'Quality Management is not a fixed body of revealed truths but a process that is evolving and will take on differing forms to meet the needs of inidividual companies. Corporations faithful to any of the three gurus have transformed their performance and become quality leaders in their own markets. Other large corporations in both the USA and the UK have intentionally utilised the advice of all the gurus, as well as other experts, with considerable success. Although the teachings of the various experts differ in content and emphasis, each has wisdom that can be included in every company's total quality management process'. International Business Machines (IBM) has been able to weld the concepts of the Gurus with their own contributions to the evolution of total quality management.

Mainly the writings of Crosby, Deming, Juran, Ishikawa, Leonard and Sausser are reviewed here. These writings are fairly representative of the fast-growing literature on quality management practices.

Crosby (1979) is best known for his focus on people oriented issues in Quality Management. He has highlighted the cultural and behavioral aspects of quality management like employee motivation and rewards. He emphasised such concepts as 'do it right first time' and 'quality is free'. Crosby (1979) gives the details of his 14 step zero-defects programme, which include management, committment, establishment of quality measurement, training, calculating the cost of quality, and error cause removal. These steps are summarised in table 2.1. (See Table on next page)

Deming (1981, 1982, 1986) approaches the problem of Quality Management from a statistician's perspective. Earlier he worked on improving quality in manufacturing through the use of statistical quality control techniques. Recently he has broadened his approach through 14 principles of quality management (Deming 1982). In these principles, emphasis is laid on strong management commitment to quality, process design and control through statistical tools, continuous search for and correction of quality problem and a purchasing policy that prefers quality over cost and schedule objectives. Deming advocates the removal of all barriers to employee participation and teamwork. The emphasis is to have effective communication between supervisors and employees, the elimination of numerical goals and quota for employees, and company wide training & education in quality. Sinha & Willborn (1985) gives the detailed description of these 14 principles of quality management, with brief explanations. Deming is strongly against motivational programmes which have little lasting effect and misunderstand the role of the worker Deming is quoted as saying "How can a man do it right first time when the incoming material is off gauge, off-colour or otherwise defective, or if his machine is not in order?" (Macdonald & Piggot, 1992).

It is directed against the misuse of zero-defects as motivational tool in the United States during the sixties. Deming's contribution to the field of quality management can be gauged by the fact that a large number of books, based on his teachings and preachings have appeared in the published form; (Mann, 1992), (Scherkenbach, 1992), (Walton, 1993 a, 1993 b).

Juran has helped in building the conceptual basis for quality management. He is considered to be one of the early leaders in the field of quality management. In 1940s he highlighted managerial responsibility for quality and emphasised that quality management was achieved through people rather than the tech-

Table 2.1 "Factors of Quality Management as highlighted by selected authors"

Critical &Factors	Adam, Herschauer & Ruch	Crosby	Deming	Garvin	Juran	Ishikawa	Leonard &	Mondon
The role of top management leadership		Management commitment,quality goal setting purpose towards	Define management's permanent commitment and obligation to implement the Demming principles. Create constancy of quality. Adopt new management philosophy towards defects, mistakes, and defective materials.	Setting quality programs and policies,attitudes of management and employees.	Upper management leadership and quality policy.	ment's strategic support for quality.	Personal concern for quality and quality conscious management style. Assign responsibility for quality. Top manage- port for quality.	Setting strategic role of quality in the organizations.
The role of the quality department		Quality councils. Quality improvement teams.			Organizational mechanism/program to improve quality.	Quality function is the responsibility of all departments.	Professional quality assurance and control staff.	Proper use of quality staff as consultants for advance quality problems, extensive training by quality professionals.
Training	Employee training and orientation.	Supervisor training and employee training.	Use modern methods of training using statistics. Institute various program of training and education.		Training,at all levels appropriate quality tools.	Training of employees in problem solving, data analysis, and statistical techniques.	Training and development of employees and management.	Quality training at all levels including top management.
Product/ defining product/	Product design, customer product	Understanding fully	through reliably	Product design emphasizing fitness	Product design		trial testing,coordin-	Product design by service

design	service quality characteristics.	and service requirements.		planning, trial production, and testing and producibility.	for use.			ation of affected departments in product/service design, selective automation.
Supplier quality management	Effective purchasing to improve quality.		Reduce suppliers, award contracts on the basis of quality. Do not choose suppliers based on cost alone.	Vendor management by streamlining vendors, long-term relationships, emphasis on quality not costs.	Vendor relations using statistical methods.			Supplier participation in quality control activities by strong, interdependent and long-term relationships.
Process management	Design and control of setup procedures. Maintenance and repair. Planning, scheduling, and control techniques and tools. Process design, location, layout job design, equipment, tooling, job enrichment.	Qualification of process. Corrective action. Zero-defect planning. Error-cause removal.	Use statistical tools in manufacturing and purchasing. Search continually for problems in the system (design, materials, machines, training, supervision). Emphasize teamwork for solving quality problems (sales, manufacturing, research, and design).	Production and work force policies, smooth production schedule.	Process design emphasizing quality planning and quality improvement.	Process improvement through problem analysis.	Organization-wide analysis of quality problems.	Statistical quality control. Participation by all departments in quality control. Autonomous process management. Selective automation of process and inspection.
Quality data and		Quality measurment. Cost of quality.	Use statistical methods to improve quality continuously.	Quality information system.	Quality information system including cost of quality, external and internal failure data.	Quality data gathering and analysis at all levels.	Quality information system for effective decision making at management and employee levels.	Cost and quality committees gather company-wide data for management analysis.
Employee relations	Participation of employees. Com-	Employee recognition. Quality awar-	Remove all barriers to worker's	Employee involvement in quality	Employee relations including quality	Employee involvement in quality problem	Open participation by employees in quality	Suggestion schemes and employee

	munication. Employee selection. Reward structure: monetary & non-monetary rewards.	eness. Zero-defect day.	pride of workmanship. Eliminate quality-related numerical goals and quotas. Modern supervision ensuring immediate action on quality problems. Encourage communication.	improvement at all levels and in all functions.	circles.	solving.	improvement.	involvement.

Source : Saraph J.V., Benson P.G., & Schroeder R.G. "An Instrument for Measuring the Critical Factors of Quality", Decision Sciences, Vol. 20 No.3 summer 89, pp. 810-829.

niques. This approach is in contrast with Deming's approach. In his writings, Juran (1970, 1974, 1978, 1981a, 1981b, 1986), stressed on both managerial and technical aspects of quality management. He proposed three basic processes which are popularly termed as Juran's trilogy. It's components are : quality control (giving conformance), quality improvement (by specific projects), and managerial and technical break throughs (quantum leaps in quality conformance). His approach emphasises quality planning, establishment of formal quality policy, quality through product design, quality audits and the systems approach to managing quality through-out the organisation. He stressed a dedication for quality at each step in the product development cycle : market research, product design, vendor relations, manufacturing, delivery and service. Juran (1974) gives the organisational requirements for effective quality management. While Deming advocates the practice of fewer suppliers, Juran is not in favour of single sourcing for key purchases. Similar view is expressed by Macdonald and Piggot (1992) :

"For important purchases it is well to use multiple sources of supply. A single source can more easily neglect to sharpen its competitive edge in quality costs and services."

Juran is in favour of Quality circles (QCs) because they improve communication between management and employees. He advocates the use of statistical process control but cautions against the use of a 'tool oriented approach'. He is of the opinion that even the largest of U.S. companies will take 8 years as against 15 years it took for Japanese companies for top-down training in quality. However Deming is not so optimistic he thinks it will take thirty years (McDonald & Piggot, 1992). Juran's prime objectives is to get top management to help the company's management team to develop the habit of continuous improvement (Ali, 1993).

Ishikawa (1976) charted the route to quality improvement through training of foreman and employees. He offerred Ishikawa-diagrams to diagnose quality problems through the use of cause & effect diagrams. He has stressed on employee participation and quality circles.

Leonard and Sasser (1982) proposed a theory of quality management based on factors that management can manipulate. These factors are termed as quality management 'levers' that management can use for improving quality. Some of these 'levers' are : top management's strategic support for quality, hiring managers with high personal concern for quality, development of professional quality assurance staff, encouragement of employee participation in quality improvement, emphasis on employee training & development, and practicing organisation-wide analysis to identify factors affecting quality. These are summarised in table 2.1.

Company wide aspects of quality management at Toyota Motor Co. were discussed by Mondon (1982). The salient features of this system are : strong upper management involvement in quality planning, integration of quality in all functions, supplier's participation in quality management practices, efficient process and product design.

Many other authors (Bain, 1982; Cole, 1980; Gitlow & Hertz, 1983; Halpin, 1966; Hostage, 1975) have offered their views on organisational requirements, which are also termed as factors, for effective quality management system. Their findings are largely experience based and are not based on empirical research. However, Garvin (1983 & 1984) developed a set of critical factors based on systematic empirical research. Garvin, in his study of window airconditioner manufacturer in the U.S. and Japan, gave the first systematic empirical study of quality management practices prevalent in the sample organisations and their impact on quality performance was studied. He concluded that the quality leader's are performing especially well in several areas of quality management. The quality leaders excell due to : strong management support, for quality, a comprehensive goal setting process, superior quality information system, thorough product design, smooth production schedules, employee training, and enlightened vendor management policies.

QUALITY MANAGEMENT PRACTICES

The American Quality Foundation, in collaboration with Ernst & Young, has embarked on a comprehensive study to examine quality management practices in 3 countries - Japan, Germany, and the US - and within 4 industries - automative, computer, health care, and banking (Hammond, 1991). The study has 4 primary objectives : 1. to develop an inventory of quality management practices used by both manufacturing and service organizations, 2. to determine which practices constitute the best practices with each industry group, as well as the practices that transcend industries, 3. to document how differing cultures influence the application of quality management practices, and 4. to identify emerging trends and new directions in the field of quality management. Preliminary results reveal that there is a consensus among countries and industries that quality stems not from single actions but from integrated, cross-functional activity across all levels in an organization. (Hammond, Joshua; 1991)

The total quality management process (TQMP) model is outlined as a development from the original idea of improving quality management process (IQMP). According to McLean and Persico (1990) the revised model is intended to overcome deficiencies in the IQMP model. The TQMP model reveals : 1. how to promote more guidance and direction to the organization involved in a quality transformation effort, 2. the role of the steering committee, 3. the importance of statistics, and 4. the role of customers and suppliers. It stresses the importance of process as a key determinant of results. The TQMP model places a greater emphasis on the need to view the organization and its practices from a process focus rather than merely an outcome or results focus. Commitment is the foundation of an effective total quality management (TQM) initiative. Leadership is the key issue in promoting commitment. Leaders must be able to inspire others to create and manage change, to take responsibility, and, above all, to take risks. Atkinson (1991) studied the influence of type of leadership on TQM initiative in an organisation.

Two types of leaders viz. transformational and transactional leaders have been considered. Transformational leaders are independent, visionary, and inspirational and are driven by long-term goals, visions, and objectives. They are interested in ends rather than means. Transactional managers, in contrast, are especially good at achieving short-term results, fostering teamwork, and working in a practical manner. Clearly, transformational leaders and transactional managers need to work together. What they do with their people will determine the success they achieve.

Some organizations may find that their quality effort is not moving as fact as they had expected or hoped, that the effort has a missing quality link. Fishman and Kavanaugh (1989) identifies this missing quality link in the supervisor's role. As the organization begins to practice total quality management (TQM), supervisors will be called upon to provide meaningful support to problem-solving teams. In order to create a climate where new ideas can take hold, the supervisor should listen to proposals with objectivity and create conditions that allow for safe risk-taking. The supervisor needs to create a climate of motivation and manage the dynamics that will build high levels of commitment in groups and individuals. In addition, continuous improvement should be encouraged and efforts given recognition. When giving feedback, supervisors should focus on a particular thing they liked. Supervisors can make or break a quality improvement effort. Building on supervisor commitment provides a stronger foundation for deploying quality management.

Three companies were surveyed by Hayes (1990) with regard to their management practices, how they put total quality management (TQM) to work, and what they expect to achieve in the coming years through the use of TQM. Ed Dunford of TRW Space & Defense Sector stated that TQM makes sense from a business standpoint - it improves quality, reduces costs, and enhances productivity. TQM cuts through cumbersome problems so that good products can be manufactured, with a potential of saving 30% and creating a pleasant workplace. A.M. Lovelace of General Dynamics believes that global competition and the increased demand for quality make TQM essential. According to Mike Wintermute of M/A-COM Government Systems Division, being a government supplier is an incentive to adopting TQM because the government requires that its suppliers use the concept. Management must let employees know it is serious about TQM.

As defined by the Japanese, quality control (QC) management involves : 1. designing for quality, 2. process control, 3. process improvement, and 4. inspection (Handfield, 1989). The Japanese applied the statistical techniques of Juran and Deming to a wide variety of areas to develop their own unique method of quality management. It was not until the late 1970s that the principles of Juran, Crosby, and Deming began to be recognized by US management. New methods of quality control used in Japan have been introduced to US assembly line workers, and the results up to the present have appeared favorable. A study was performed by Ebrahimpour and Lee (1988) of quality improvement programs (QIP) in electronic manufacturing firms operating in the US. These firms were divided into 3 types : 1. American firms using the traditional approach to quality management (Type A), 2. Japanese firms operating in the US (Type B), and 3. American firms using some type of Japanese approach to quality management (Type C). Case studies of 10 electronic manufacturing firms provide specific suggestions for improving quality, enhancing productivity, and increasing market share and profits. Commitment and support for QIP varied among types. Top managers of Type A firms called quality an important organizational and strategic tool but did little to show their support and commitment to QIP. Type B and C firm managers directly managed and led QIP. Type A managers also showed less commitment to change corporate culture to create a quality-oriented culture. Quality control (QC) departments had less interaction with other employees in Type A firms, while in Type B and C, everyone was encouraged to become involved in QC activities. The failure of government productivity efforts to improve the quality of public service has prompted calls for the complete overhaul of management procedures. Total quality management (TQM) is a theory-based option that allows public managers to reward truly exceptional individual performance while increasing the capacity for agency-wide cooperation and process improvement. Milakovich (1991) attempts to apply W. Edwards Deming's 14-point TQM philosophy to the public sector by : 1. creating and publishing to all employees a statement of the aims and purposes of the organization, 2. understanding the purpose of inspection for improvement of processes and reduction of cost, 3. ending the practice of awarding business on the basis of price alone, 4. constantly improving the system of production and service, 5. teaching and instituting leadership, 6. creating a climate for innovation, and 7. eliminating numerical quotas for production.

Wolf and Hurtado (1990) conducted a survey to determine current quality management practices on the project management level. Data was derived from interviews with 71 major organizations and the survey answers of 41 other firms were used to determine current quality management practice on the project management level, the difficulties encountered in the implementation of quality management programs, and the opinions on how project quality can be enhanced. Results indicate that:

1. there is a wide and growing awareness of the need for quality performance, and considerable effort is being expanded in order to achieve it,
2. the specific techniques being used are project-phase-rather than whole-project-oriented, and
3. with respect to quality performance, engineering and design are considered the best-and construction the worst-project component.

The responding firms concluded that, although much can be done by those on the operating level in project management to increase project quality, their effectiveness is contingent on top management support and sufficient available resources. It was suggested that greater efforts should be made to determine and control the cost of project quality.

Allen and Oakland (1988, 1991a, 1991b) conducted a 3-stage project on the practice of quality management in the UK textile industry. The first stage of a research project concerned with an examination of the practice of quality management in the UK's textile industry sought to examine quality management practices in view of company background. One hundred eighty three textile companies responded to the postal questionnaire survey. The results indicate that, in some areas, quality management in the textile industry is less well developed than in others. The findings confirm that the implementation of documented quality systems influences performance in other areas of quality management. Some 88% of respondents claimed to have a management representative responsible for quality, but only 54% had a separate quality control and assurance department. Only 27% said a quality manual existed in the company. Specifications for all finished products were present in 64% of the companies. In the second stage of a 3-stage project on the practice of quality management in the UK textile industry, structured in-company interviews were conducted in 23 organizations with the quality manager or inspector (Allen and Oakland 1991a). Of those interviewed, 96% thought that their senior colleagues placed an important emphasis on quality. However, only 2 of the 23 companies had formulated a quality policy, and only 5 had written corrective action procedures to deal with rejected material or other quality problems. In all, 19 firms inspected supplied goods on receipt, and 15 of these controlled the quality of the incoming goods by randomly selecting a sample and inspecting it. The most popular method to detect faults during process control was the operator carrying out a visual inspection while patrolling the production machinery. For final inspection, the most popular technique was 100% inspection. According to Allen & Oakland (1991a) inspite of a general increase in awareness of the importance of quality to competitiveness, actual management practices in the textile industry have not changed greatly.

In the third stage out of the 23 companies taking part in an earlier survey, 5 agreed to further work (Allen and Oakland 1991b). A researcher visited the respondent's factory sites and assessed the existing quality systems. The basis for the assessment of the quality systems was BS 5750 Part 2 (ISO 9002). A semi-quantitative analysis of the in-company work was conducted based on a new method for rating quality management systems. This involved using "experts" to rank company profiles synthesized from various quality system attributes and subjecting the results to conjoint analysis. The results of this work indicated that there is a lack of good quality management practices within the textile industry in the UK.

Research was conducted by Instone and Dale (1989) in an organization that markets, designs, manufactures, and installs bread-making equipment to determine whether or not quality improvement is necessary, and how the present quality system could be developed. The need for quality improvement was highlighted by : 1. Quality problems would manifest themselves on a daily basis with shortages of parts, machine shop work backlog, and rescheduling of jobs. 2. Competitive companies had formulated quality objectives, strategies, and plans. 3. The sales figures were expected to triple within the next few years. 4. Managers had taken actions on quality, causing an upward pressure on senior management to create a quality management culture. Senior management needs to take the lead if any quality initiative is to be credible and effective. The attitudes of individuals are a key issue for quality improvement. Various ways to increase quality awareness are suggested by the authors.

QUALITY & PRODUCTIVITY

Deming (1982) discusses what top management must do to improve both quality and productivity. His 14-points serve as a guidelines for management in this direction. Deming's answer to the question of why productivity increases with improvement of quality is very practical : "less rework". Sinha and Willborn

(1985) suggest that higher quality and resulting enhanced customer satisfaction and sales normally also increase productivity. According to them in 1981 a survey of 197 corporate executives was undertaken which showed that the respondents do not generally understand the relationship between quality and productivity. When asked what critical issues they were facing, 82% ranked productivity as the top issue and 68% said the quality is also a critical issue.

Raman (1985) discusses with various examples the relationship between quality and productivity. Both have a major role to play in the economic development of the country. It is emphasised that productivity can be improved through quality. Edosomwan (1987) highlights various benefits that can be derived from implementing Productivity & Quality Management. Further he presents twelve causes for decline of productivity in organisations, and concludes with saying that the same reasons are applied to the decline of quality within organisations.

India lags behind many other nations with respect to productivity in manufacturing sector. This productivity gap can be filled by quantum jumps in productivity levels (Singh, 1989). Failure of managements to keep pace with changes affecting the jobs, work places, lack of flexibility, information sharing and lack of new ideas within the organisation are key inhibitors to achieving higher productivity (Singh, 1991).

According to Chatterjee (1993) quality and productivity are not tradeoffs. The aim of productivity is to produce better and not necessarily produce more. High quality of products results in better output fewer rejects, lesser rework, less wastage, lower cost and therefore levels of productivity are increased (Chatterjee, 1993).

The same view point is corroborated by the findings of Singh (1993). Quality contributes to productivity improvement and is a sure way to higher productivity.

Ghosh & Vihari (1994) studied the multi dimensional aspect of technology, quality and productivity. They propose a synergistic approach to get the best results. They offer salient practical tips on technology and quality management in the Indian context.

STUDIES IN INDIAN CONTEXT

The available literature on quality management practices in the Indian context is sketchy and scattered. Many authors have contributed theoretical and informative articles on the subject matter of Total Quality Management, Quality Management and ISO-9000 series. The research papers based on empirical data are few. Some case studies on successful implementation of Total Quality Management in various business organisations have appeared in the published form. The literature is reviewed here in the Indian context from company wide managerial point of view.

Patel (1971) gave theoretical aspects of quality control in industrial products. The importance and benefits of product quality are highlighted in order to remain viable in the competitive world. Raman (1978) developed strategies, both at macro and micro level, for improving quality of Indian products. He gave a good account of quality control status against the prevailing economic and industrial background. According to him quality control in various organisations has not found adequate place though inspection aspects have somewhat been appreciated. Srinivasan (1982) studied the price-quality interface and offered a selling strategy for field sales force in the wake of competition from cheap and spurious goods manufacturers. He studied the economic and psychological impact of price-quality dimension on the customer. He concluded by offering a set of guidelines to the salesforce wherein it is suggested to highlight the benefits of price over cost.

Sahu (1987) discusses the relevance of quality and offers a strategy for the growth of quality movement. He lays emphasis on quality control circles. The strategy includes attention on education & training for personnel, R&D efforts, decentralised and participative management styles, etc. Samat (1987) based on his experience of working in BHEL, focussed on the quality aspects in managing an engineering enterprise. According to him practices like setting up of quality circles will ensure involvement of workers in the quality management. He throws light on various quality management practices being followed in BHEL plants, prominent among them are : training, quality circles, quality improvement projects, subcontractor's quality development and customer service. Raju (1987) studied the role of top management in following sound quality management practices, with special reference to electronics and communication industry both in public and private sector. He suggested the kind of measure to be implemented by the management. Raju (1987) reiterates that active involvement of top management in quality management practices is necessary. According to him, the aspects of involvement of top management are : provision of resources, prompt correction of system's weakness and promotion of positive attitudinal change to trigger and sustain improvement. Bidhichand (1990) examined both theoretically and empirically whether public sector undertakings are weak in terms of quality and, therefore, require privatisation from this point of view. This examination has been restricted to the quality of services offered by export trade organisations and road passenger transport undertakings in the public sector. The results of this examination shows that public enterprises in these two areas fared quite well, in terms of quality control.

Lal (1990) highlights the importance of human factor in quality management. The attitudes of top management and operators have been described in detail and a few tips are given to the management for motivating the workforce. Singh (1991) undertook a survey for understanding the concept and practices of total quality management in selected public and private sector organisations. Role of top and middle management in adopting good quality management practices is elucidated. Response was received from 52 organisations where in Total Quality Management (TQM) is under implementation. The questionnaires were analysed with a view to find out the quality management practices in Indian organisations. Finally, some problems and pitfalls in implementing TQM have been discussed.

Chandna (1992) raises apprehensions about whether TQM will succeed in India. Various pitfalls in implementing total quality management are highlighted and an attempt has been made to evaluate each of these pitfalls and their impact. Finally, preventive steps have been suggested to enable Indian companies gain global superiority in quality and productivity. Paramesvar (1993) examined many facets of the key role played by standardization in real industrial life. Implications of rapid technological developments has also been discussed. Singh (1993 b) discussed various aspects of quality policy and corporate vision which lead to the creation of a healthy organisation culture. He concluded by highlighting the importance of top management's backing to the TQM initiative. He asserts that implementation of TQM and analysis of its impact on organisations is achieved gradually.

Singh (1993 a) elucidated the rules of the game in the world economic scenario and concluded that TQM is the only strategy for emerging victorious in the economic battlefield. It is equally useful in large or small organisations, manufacturing or service organisations, and public or private organisations. Chakraborty (1993) suggests a shift in strategy to be adopted by management in the wake of continuously changing dynamic world of industry. According to him the management should concentrate on intangibles such as better quality, greater flexibility, faster time to market, quicker order processing, improved vendor relations and higher customer satisfaction. Senior managers at Voltas proceeded systematically with the objective of 'market leadership through continuous quality improvement process'. An apex quality council was formed which sought professional assistance from various agencies such as Confederation of Indian Industries, Quality Circles Forum of India, Qimpro and ICA. As a result three of their business units were given the distinction of ISO 9001 certification (Singh, 1993).

Sharad (1993) provides some linkages between TQM & Management by Projects (MBP) with particular emphasis on construction industry. Bhaskaran (1993) discussed the importance of quality in marketing and influence of quality on the customer. The importance of Quality Management is evident from the fact that the Anna University proposes to establish a centre for quality management to improve quality awareness and consciouness among the people (-,1994).

Some case studies on implementation of TQM in leading Indian business organisations have appeared in the published form. Gondhalekar and others have studied the behavioral aspects of productivity improvement through the application of TQM in Godrej (Gondhalekar et.al., 1991). The Godrej-Kaizen system was developed and its impact on attitudinal changes in the employees was studied. It was concluded that the Kaizen system drastically reduces resistance to change Shekhar (1991) studied the quality improvement process in Modi Xerox. Sharma and Gupta (1992) studied the application of TQM in Samtel Colour Ltd. They engineered changes in inspection system and measured its impact on over all performance of the organisation, with a view to achieve high levels of customer satisfaction, increase in output, and reduction in rejects. The impact of modified system was analysed on various performance parameters. It was observed that the modified system caused improvements in all the performance parameters. Ramesh & Gowda (1992) shares the experience of Kirloskar Electric's unit III plant at Bangalore, in adopting and practicing TQM in 1985. They concluded by highlighting both tangible and intangible benefits of implementing TQM.

A Quality Circle group has been created in 1982 to coordinate and guide the activities of Quality Circles and its 15 chapter around the country have been vigorously conducting different kinds of programmes and bringing out numerous publications on this topic. Some two hundred organisations are registered with this body (Jain 1990).

The International Convention on Quality Control Circle Organised in Dec. 1989 and The National Convention on Quality Circle organised in Hyderabad in Dec. 1990 by Quality Circle Forum of India are important milestone in the progress of the movement (Udpa 1990).

Status report of Quality Circle in India estimated about 370 companies equally divided between public and private enterprises are practicing Quality Circle (Srinivasan 1991).

Quality Circle activities were brought to India by the Bharat Heavy Electricals Limited (BHEL) Ramchandrapuram unit at Hyderabad (Srinivasan 1991). Quality Circles were started in its plant with five circles in 1981. Now this movement has grown to 1,629 circles in 1990 spread over its plants at Bhopal, Hyderabad, Hardwar, Trichi and Bangalore.

Indian Railways which is the largest government owned organisation in our country, with nearly 1.6 million employees, joined the Quality Circle movement in the later part of 1987. There are about 400 Quality Circle groups functioning in Railways (Srinivasan 1991).

REFERENCES

Ali, A., 1993. "Total Quality Management". Indian Management, Feb.-March, pp 53 - 57.

Allen, Neal and Oakland, J.S., 1988. "Quality Assurance in the Textile Industry : Part I". International Journal of Quality and Reliability Management, Vol. 5, Iss. 5, pp. 25 - 37.

Allen, Neal and Oakland, J.S., 1991a. "Quality Assurance in the Textile Industry : Part II". International Journal of Quality and Reliability Management, Vol. 8, Iss. 1, pp. 22 - 30.

Allen, Neal and Oakland, J.S., 1991b. "Quality Assurance in the Textile Industry : Part III". International Journal of Quality and Reliability Management, Vol. 8, Iss. 2, pp. 9 - 20.

Atkinson, P., 1991. "Leadership; Total Quality and Cultural Change" Management Services, Vol. 35, Iss : 6, June, pp. 16 - 19.

Bain, D.L., 1982. The Productivity Prescription. New York : McGraw-Hill.

Bidhichand, 1990. "Quality Control As a Method of Enhancing Competitiveness of Public Sector and its Privatisation", in Om Prakash (Ed) Public Sector At the Cross roads, Jaipur : RBSA Publishers, pp 187 - 200.

Chakraborty, S. 1993. "Is Indian Management Really Committed to Quality". Indian Management, Vol. 32, No. 2 & 3, February-March, pp. 47 - 52.

Chandna, J.K., 1992. "Will Total Quality Management succeed in India ?" The Economic Times, November 19, p. 13.

Chatterjee, P.K., 1993. "Quality Excellence for Productivity Improvement". Productivity, Vol. 34, No. 2, Jul-Sept., pp. 288 - 291.

Cole, R.E., 1980. "Learning from the Japanese". Management Review, 69(9), pp 22-42.

Crosby, P.B., 1979. Quality Is Free. New York : New American Library.

Deming, W.E., 1981. "Improvement of Quality and Productivity Through Action by Management". National Productivity Review, 1(1), pp 12-22.

Deming, W.E., 1982. Quality, Productivity and Competitive Position. Cambridge, MA : MIT Center for Advanced Engineering.

Deming, W.E., 1986. Out of the crisis. Cambridge, MA : MIT Center for Advanced Engineering.

Ebrahimpour, M. and Lee, S.M., 1988. "Quality Management Practices of American and Japanese Electronic Firms in the United States". Production and Inventory Management, Vol. 29, Iss. 4, pp. 28 - 31.

Edosomwan, J.A., 1987. Integrating Productivity and Quality Management, New-York. Marcel Dekker Inc, pp. 11-13.

Fishman, N. and Kavanaugh, L., 1989. "Searching for your Missing Quality Link". Journal for Quality and Participation, Dec., pp. 28 - 32.

Garvin, D.A., 1983. "Quality on the line". Harvard Business Review, 61(5), pp 65-75.

Garvin, D.A., 1984. "Japanese quality management". Columbia Journal of World Business, 19(3), pp 3-12.

Ghosh, S. and Vihari, V., 1994. "Technology, Quality and Productivity" in Gupta, N.K. and Ahmad, A. (Eds.) Managing Transition, New Delhi : Wiley Eastern Ltd., pp. 102 - 110.

Gitlow, H.S., & Hertz, P.T., 1983. "Product defects and productivity". Harward Business Review, 61(5), pp 131-141.

Goetz, V.J., 1978. Quality Assurance : A Program for Whole Organization. New York : AMACOM, American Management Association.

Gondhalekar, S., Tripathi, A., and Hombali, S., 1991. "The Godrej Kaizen System : Company Wide Productivity Improvement". Productivity, Vol. 32, No. 3, October-December, pp. 450-457.

Halpin, J.F., 1966. Zero Defects. New York : McGraw-Hill. Hammond, Joshua, 1991. "An International Look at Quality Practices". Management Review, Vol. 80, Iss. 5, May, pp. 38 - 41.

Handfield, R., 1989. "Quality Management in Japan versus the United States : An Overview". Production & Inventory Management, Vol. 30, Iss. 2, pp. 79 - 85.

Hayes, G.E., 1990. "Three Views of T.Q.M.". Quality, Vol. 29, Iss. 4, April, pp. 19 - 24.

Hostage, G.M., 1975. "Quality Control in Service Business". Harward Business Review, 53(4), pp 98-106.

Inston, F.J. and Dale, B.G., 1989. "A Case Study of the Typical Issues Involved in Quality Improvement". International Journal of Operations and Production Management, Vol. 9, Iss. 1, pp. 15 - 26.

Ishikawa, K., 1976. Guide to Quality Control. Tokyo : Asian Productivity Organization.

Jain, R.K., 1990. "Impact of QC on Organisational Culture", (Proceedings of International Convention on Quality Control Circles, New Delhi, India, Dec 6-9 1989). In Excellence Through Participation, New Delhi, Tata McGraw Hill Publishing Co. Ltd.

Juran, J.M., 1974. Quality Control Handbook (3rd Ed.). New York : McGraw-Hill.

Juran, J.M., 1978. "Japanese and Western Quality : A Contrast in Methods and Results". Management Review, 67(11), pp 27-45.

Juran, J.M., 1981a. "Product Quality - A Prescription for the West, Part I". Management Review, 70(6), pp 8-14.

Juran, J.M., 1981b. "Product Quality - A Prescription for the West, Part II". Management Review, 70(7), pp 57-61.

Juran, J.M., 1986. "The Quality Trilogy". Quality Progress, 9(8), pp 19-24.

Juran, J.M., & Gryna, F.M., Jr., 1970. Quality Planning and Analysis. New York : McGraw-Hill.

Lal, H., 1990. Total Quality Management - A Practical Approach, New Delhi : Wiley-Eastern Ltd., pp. 58-62.

Leonard, F.S., & Sasser, W.E., 1982. "The Incline of Quality". Harward Business Review, 60(5), pp 163-171.

Macdonald, J. and Piggott, J., 1992. Global Quality The New Management Culture, New Delhi : Viva Books Pvt. Ltd., p. 92.

Main, Jeramy, 1986. "Under the Spell of the Gurus", Fortune, August.

Mann, N.R., 1992. The Keys to Excellence - The Deming Philosophy, New Delhi : Viva Books Pvt. Ltd.

McLean, G.N. and Persico, J., 1990. "An Updated Model for Implementing a Quality and Productivity System". Journal of Managerial Psychology, Vol. 5, Iss. 1, pp. 23 - 32.

Milakovich, M.E., 1991. "Total Quality Management in the Public Sector". National Productivity Review, Vol. 10, Iss. 2, pp. 195 - 213.

Mondon, Y., 1982. Toyota Production System. New York : American Institute of Industrial Engineers.

Paramesvar, K.R., 1993. "Role of Standards in Technology Management". Productivity, Vol. 33, No. 4, Jan-March, pp. 596 - 600.

Patel, D.M., 1971. "Quality Control in Industrial Products". Productivity, Vol. XII, No. 2, pp. 444-448.

Raju, S.M. Sundara, 1987. "Quality & Top Management", Productivity, Vol 27, No. 4, pp. 377 - 380.

Raman, M.V.V., 1978. "Strategy for Improving Quality of Indian Products". Productivity, April-June, pp. 23 - 32.

Raman, M.V.V., 1985. "Quality-Productivity Interface". Productivity, XXV, 4, pp. 475 - 479.

Ramesh, S. and Gowda, V., 1992. "Kirloskar Electric Route Map to TQM". Productivity, Vol. 33, No. 1, April-June, pp. 141 - 149.

Sahu, K.C., 1987. "Quality Changing Concept and Scope". Productivity, Vol. 28, No. 1, April-June, pp. 17-25.

Samat, B.S., 1987. "Quality Management in an Indian Engineering Enterprise". Productivity, Vol. 27, No. 4, pp. 327 - 334.

Scherkenbach, W.W., 1992. The Deming Routeto Quality and Productivity - Road Maps and Road Blocks, New Delhi: Viva Books Pvt. Ltd.

Sharad, D., 1993. "Total Quality Management Through MBP". Indian Management, Feb. - March, pp. 58 - 61.

Sharma, I.M. and R.S. Gupta, 1991. "TQM in Samtel Color Ltd." Productivity, Vol. 32, No. 3, October-December, pp. 467 - 471.

Shekar, R., 1991. "Modi Xerox Implementation Process Strategy and Elements". Productivity, Vol. 32, No.3, October-December, pp. 458 - 466.

Singh, A., 1989. "Status of Quality Circles in India". Productivity, Jan-March.

Singh, A., 1991. "Total Quality Management : Concept and Practice in India". Productivity, Vol. 32, No.3, October-December, pp. 393 - 399.

Singh, A. 1993a. "Quality & the Competitive Environment". Productivity, Vol. 34, No.3, October-December, pp. 431 - 436.

Singh, A. 1993b. "Corporate Vision and Quality Policy : Creating an organisation culture". Productivity, Vol. 33, No. 4, Jan-March 1993.

Singh, B., 1993. "Transformational Leadership". Economic Times, New Delhi : December 21, p. 8.

Sinha, M.N. and Willborn, W., 1985. The Management of Quality Assurance, New York : John Wiley and Sons, p. 73.

Srinivasan, A.V., 1991. "Quality Circle movement in India : A status report". ASCI Journal of Management, Vol. 21, No. 1, June, pp. 21 - 46.

Udpa, S.R., 1990. "Quality Circles for the growth in the 90's". Indian Express, Oct. 15, p. 6.

Walton, M., 1993a. The Deming Management Method - The Complete Guide to Quality Management, New Delhi : Viva Books Pvt. Ltd.

Walton, M. 1993b. Deming Management At Work, New Delhi : Viva Books Pvt. Ltd.

Wolf, C. and Hurtado, Y.C., 1990. "Quality Management Practice in Capital Projects". A.A.C.E. Transitions, pp. Q. 4.1 - Q. 4.8.

----, 1994. "Quality Management Centre". University News, September 12, pp. 21 - 22.

CHAPTER 3

RESEARCH METHODOLOGY

In the beginning of this chapter rationale of the study is established, followed by statement of the problem, scope & objectives of the study, operational definitions of terms used in the study have been given. In the next sections, research design, sampling design, procedure for data collection and the questionnaire has been described in detail. Finally, aspects like analysis and interpretation of the collected data and inherent limitations of the study have been highlighted.

RATIONALE OF THE STUDY

Various studies mentioned in the preceding chapter clearly point out that not much work has been carried out to determine quality management practices in organisations. Numerous studies conducted abroad are largely meant for specific industries such as textile, electronics, etc. Quality management practice of Japanese and United States firms have been compared. Saraph et al (1989) have developed an instrument for measuring Quality Management Practices.

In the Indian context mainly case studies on implementation of total quality management (TQM) have been conducted. In some studies attempts have been made to link quality with a single variable such as price or productivity. No study has come to the notice of the researcher, which attempts to assess quality management practices in a cross section of industries, except that of Singh (1991). As a result, the present study has been pursued.

It is probably the first time that a general focus is placed on studying quality management practices of a cross section of industries. The empirical research in Madhya Pradesh in this area has been found to be wanting. Production and quality management are basically applied disciplines, therefore close interactions with practioners in the field is necessary.

Quality management has become very crucial to the survival of industry. Quality assumes greater significance in the light of following factors : (a) increased customer quality requirements, (b) which leads to current practices being out model, and (c) the emphasis on cost reduction. The domestic market is becoming more competitive because of recent economic policies of the Government. Overseas buyers had been skeptical of 'Made in India' Label. Hence Indian business organisations are in dire need of improving quality of their operations and also a globally accepted certificate of reliability in order to survive. It has therefore become imperative that current status of quality management practices be explored in manufacturing organisations.

STATEMENT OF THE PROBLEM

The present study is an attempt to encompass various aspects of the basic problem which is stated as follows :

"A study of the Quality Management Practices in Selected Organisations of Madhya Pradesh"

SCOPE OF THE STUDY

The study is limited to the investigations in the quality systems of manufacturing organisations only. Major emphasis is placed on studying the nature and level of quality management practices. Basically, it is intended to explore what are the current quality management practices in selected manufacturing organisations. The geographical coverage is restricted to the state of Madhya Pradesh. Small scale Industries (SSI) are excluded from the scope of the study, as many SSI's may not have a formal quality management system.

OBJECTIVES OF THE STUDY

The main objective of this study is to explore and understand the Quality Management Practices which are prevalent in selected manufacturing organisations of Madhya Pradesh.

STATEMENT OF THE OBJECTIVES

1. To study the current quality management practices in selected manufacturing organisations.
2. To seek opinions of managers in the quality/production area regarding the critical factors of quality management and to develop a measure of quality management practices.
3. To study the influence of size of organisation (a company characteristic) on quality management practices.
4. To study the influence of age of organisation (a company characteristic) on quality management practices.
5. To study the influence of type of organisation on quality management practices.

OPERATIONAL DEFINITIONS

Dr. Deming (1986) devotes an entire chapter to the topic of operational definitions in his book "Out of the Crisis". He defines operational definition as follows :

"An operational definition puts communicable meaning into a concept".

Sink (1991) highlights the importance of operational definitions in the following words :

"It appears to me that much of the confusion and disagreement regarding productivity, quality, quality of work life, total quality management, quality circles etc. arise due to the lack of operational definitions for these terms, concepts, and approaches/techniques. I believe we must begin with operational definitions for and understanding of performance and the sub-dimensions that make it up."

According to Emory and Cooper (1991) an operational definition is one stated in terms of specific testing criteria or operations. These terms must have empirical referrents..mb8

Operational definition of following terms have been given below, which are extensively used in this study :

1. **Manufacturing Organisation :** In the context of the present study, it refers to creation of goods only.
2. **Quality :** The totality of features and characteristics of a product or service that bear on its ability to satisfy stated or implied needs. In the context of the present study, it refers to characteristics of a product only.
3. **Quality Management :** That aspect of the overall management function that determines and implements quality policy.
4. **Quality System :** The organizational structure, responsibilities, procedures, processes, and resources for implementing quality management.
5. **Accreditation :** Certification by a duly recognized body of the facilities, capability, objectivity, competence, and integrity of an agency, service or operational group or individual to provide the specific service(s) or operation(s) needed.
6. **Conformance :** An affirmative indication or judgement that a product or service has met the requirements of the relevant specifications, contract, or regulation; also the state of meeting requirements.
7. **Traceability :** The ability to trace the history, application, or location of an item or activity and like items or activities by means of recorded identification.
8. **Organisation Size :** In the context of the present study, size is a function of number of employees in the organisation. Organisations having 500 or more employees are considered large organisations. While, organisations having less than 500 employees are considered as small sized organisations.
9. **Organisation age :** In the context of the present study, age is a function of number of years an organisation is in existence. Those organisations which are in existence for the last 10 or more years are considered as old organisations. While, those organisations which are in existence for less than 10 years are considered as new organisations.

10. **Type of Industry :** For the purpose of the present study, five types of industries have been included in the sample. These are Engineering, Pharmaceuticals and Chemicals, Electrical & Electronics, Agro based and Textiles industries.

Following are the specifically devised research terms for the purpose of this study :

1. Quality Management Practices Score (Aggregate) : A numerical score calculated on the basis of factors indicated by respondents on a five point Likert type of scale. A high numerical score indicates comparatively better level of Quality Management Practices prevalent in that organisation.
2. Quality Management Practices Score (Factor-wise) : The Quality Management Practices Score for each of the 8 factors that constitute quality management practices.

RESEARCH DESIGN

The research design choosen for the present study is an exploratory type. The major objective of the study is to explore what is currently happening with respect to quality management practices. Since an exploratory type of research design is framed a large number of manufacturing organisations representing a cross-section of industries are approached. Survey method is used for data collection.

SAMPLING PROCEDURE

The present study is confined to manufacturing organisations located in the state of Madhya Pradesh. There are 618 (Industrial Compendium, 1993) large and medium size organisations in Madhya Pradesh. A list of these organisations is the sampling frame for this study. The nature of research design is such that non probability sampling procedure is followed. Under this, purposive sampling has been done based on convenience and judgement.

In the first instance the questionnaire was mailed to all the 618 organisations listed in the sampling frame. Along with the questionnaire a covering letter was sent which assured the respondents that the information provided by them will be kept strictly confidential and will be used only for the purpose of analysis in the present study (Appendix A & B). Response rate was very poor as only 5 partially filled up questionnaires were received. This compelled the researcher to change the strategy, and take help from friends, acquaintances, ex-students, relatives who have some contacts in the industrial organisation's of Madhya Pradesh. The managers/executives of manufacturing organisations were personnally approached. This approach proved more fruitful than the mail survey method. The process of primary data collection was arduous as the response could be received only after repeated visits and reminders through telephone or messengers. A filled up questionnaire could be received only after visiting 4-5 times on an average. Many a times a questionnaire had to be replaced as it was reported to be missing.

Only one questionnaire was to be received from each organisation and view point of the manager incharge of Quality Management was sought. The choice of Quality Manager as the respondents from Quality management Department is based on the thinking that he is the only appropriate person in the department to be able to give information regarding policies and intimate activities in his department. In case of organisations where no manager/ executive is responsible for the quality department (in very few cases) the production manager was requested to respond to the questionnaire. The response has been received from 50 organisations. Out of this 3 responses were unusable as information on vital questions was missing. The list of 47 organisations, which is the sample for this study, is included in the appendix C.

The response pattern is depicted below in Table 3.1, which gives region-wise percent of response to contacted organisations/ persons.

Table 3.1 : Response Pattern (Region wise)

Region	No. of Respondents Contacted	Responded	% of response to contacted
1) Western Madhya Pradesh	152	30	19.74
2) Eastern South Eastern Madhya Pradesh	47	9	19.15
3) Central/Northern M.P	51	8	15.69

As is clear from the above table the response rate has been less than 20%.

PROCEDURE FOR DATA COLLECTION

Data has been collected both from secondary and primary sources.

SECONDARY DATA

Various published sources have been tapped for gathering secondary data. Data from number of research papers, books, hand-books, government reports has been collected with a view to develop conceptual frame work. This data has also been used for the review of literature. Useful information about factors and other related aspects of Quality Management could be developed. Some of the prominent libraries visited by the researcher are, Indian Institute of Management (IIM), Calcutta; American Centre library, Bombay; Jamnalal Bajaj Institute of Management studies, Bombay; Indira Gandhi Institute of Development Research, Bombay; National Productivity council, New Delhi; All India Management Association, New Delhi; and Indian Institute of Technology, New Delhi. The researcher availed of 'Online Search Database' facility at Indian Institute of Management Calcutta's library. With the help of this facility abstracts of 21 research papers in the specific area of Quality Management Practices were made available.

COLLECTION OF PRIMARY DATA

The primary data has been collected through the structured questionnaire during December 1993 to April 1994. Above mentioned sampling procedure has been followed and the response received from 47 organisations.

THE DEVELOPMENT OF AN INSTRUMENT

An instrument has been developed which attempts to measure a profile of the business unit's actual level of quality management practices. For developing this instrument the researcher relied on the study conducted by Saraph et al (1989). He has studied the quality management practices in United States based manufacturing and service organisations. The instrument developed for the present study reflects Indian conditions and realities as it was pretested among Indian professionals. Their view points on quality management practices have been incorporated. Some basic elements of quality management system have been included in the instrument, which are essentially present in organisations of industrially developed countries. For developing measures of the critical factors of quality management, a nine-step process, described by Saraph et al (1989), has been followed. Fifty three measures in the form of statements were identified as a result of literature search. After prolonged and intensive discussions with the research supervisor, colleagues, and academicians, the number was brought down to 44 statements. The instrument was, then pretested among ten quality/production managers. They were requested to comment on the following aspects of the statements (items) : appropriateness, ease of comprehension, readability, wording etc. As a result an inventory of 37 statements has been retained. To enable respondents to indicate the degree of each practice in their organisation, a six-point interval rating scale is used. To quantify the responses following scale is used.

The extent for prevailing practice is :

	Not Applicable	Very low	Low	Medium	High	Very High
Letter Code	A	B	C	D	E	F
Numerical Score	0	1	2	3	4	5

The option 'Not Applicable' has been given a numerical score of zero for computational convenience.

These 37 statements were then grouped into 8 categories which are termed as the factors of quality management practices. This grouping is similar to the grouping performed by Saraph et al (1989). Table 3.2 provides brief descriptions of these factors. .rm110

Table 3.2 : Critical factors of quality management

Critical Factors of Quality Management	Explanation of Critical Factors
1. The role of management leadership and quality policy	Acceptance of quality responsibility by General Motors' and department heads. Evaluation of top management on quality. Participation by top management in quality improvement efforts. Specificity of quality goals. Importance attached to quality in relation to cost and schedule. Comprehensive quality planning.
2. Role of the quality department	Visibility and autonomy of the quality department. The quality department's access to top management. Use of quality staff for consoltion. Coordination between quality department and other departments. Effectiveness of the quality department.
3. Training	Provision of statistical training, trade training, and quality-related training for all employees.
4. Product/service design	Thorough scrub-down process. Involvement of all affected departments in design reviews. Emphasis on productivity. Clarity of specifications. Emphasis on quality, not roll-out schedule. Avoidance of frequent redesigns.
5. Supplier quality management	Fewer dependable suppliers. Reliance on supplier process control. Strong interdependence of supplier and customer. Purchasing policy emphasizing quality rather than price. Supplier

	quality control. Supplier assistance in product development.
6. Process management	**Clarity of process ownership, boundaries, and steps. Less reliance on inspection. Use of statistical process control. Selective automation. Foolproof process design. Preventative maintenance. Employee self-inspection. Automated testing.**
7. Quality data and reporting	**Use of quality cost data. Feedback of quality data to employees and managers for problem solving. Timely quality measurement. Evaluation of managers and employees based on quality performance. Availability of quality data.**
8. Employee relations	**Implementation of employee involvement and quality circles. Open employee participation in quality decisions. Responsibility of employees for quality. Employee recognition for superior quality performance. Effectiveness of supervision in handling quality issues. On-going quality awareness of all employees.**

The reliability of the instrument was measured by the internal consistency method (Nunnally, 1981). Cronbach's coefficient alpha is calculated for the scale based on given sets of items to estimate the internal consistency. Cronbach's coefficient alpha has the most utility for multi-item scales at the interval level of measurement (Emory & Cooper, 1991). The calculated value of alpha came to be .71 for this instrument which is considered adequate, therefore the instrument is judged to be reliable. The validity of the instrument refers to the extent to which it measures what it is intended to measure. The content validity of the instrument was established by the general agreement among the academicians and practioners that this instrument cover all the aspects of quality management practices.

THE QUESTIONNAIRE

A structured questionnaire was framed to meet specific requirements of the present study. The design of the questionnaire has been kept simple. Both close and open ended questions have been included. A large number of questions are close ended while a few questions in the end are kept open-ended to seek respondent's suggestions and opinion about quality management practices. For all the close ended questions clear cut instructions have been provided at appropriate places to avoid ambiguity. The questionnaire has four parts. A brief discussion of all the four parts is given below :

Part A seeks to gather personal information about the respondent like name, designation, department, age, professional experience, educational qualifications and area/s of work. Part B deals with information regarding particulars of the organisation. Those questions have been included which aim to elicit response about the names of major products, rated and achieve capacity, sales turnover for three preceding financial years, number of employees, type of production processes, number of shifts operated and whether the organisation has single or multiple plant. In addition to the above, the information about the standard/s which is/are applicable is sought and finally the progress for obtaining certification for the above standard/s is assessed.

Part C of the questionnaire contains the instrument which has been developed in section 3.9.1.

In part D of the questionnaire some close ended questions have been included to seek additional information about quality management practices. The questions are aimed to elicit information about practices such as frequency of stoppage of production due to non conformance, quality manager's access to the top management, facilitating environmental factors for quality management and inspection related practices. Towards the end of the questionnaire opinion of the respondents is sought on effectiveness of the quality department of the organisation on a five point scale. Finally, some open-ended questions are included to seek suggestions on quality management related issues.

ANALYSIS AND PRESENTATION

The filled up questionnaires were coded and master data sheet was prepared. The data was tabulated and classified on the basis of company characteristics such as age and type of organisations to fulfil the objectives of the study. The following scoring procedure has been devised for quantifying the response to the part C, i.e. the instrument, of the questionnaire:

Aggregate score of an individual organisation was calculated by adding the item scores for all the applicable statements and this is termed as Quality Management Practices Score (QMPS). The median value of aggregate QMP scores was calculated and those organisations whose QMP score was less than the median value were termed as organisations having lower level of quality management practices, and the organisations whose QMP score was either equal or higher to the median score were termed as organisations having higher level of quality management practices. Factor wise scores have also been calculated by summing the item score for all the statements pertaining to that factor.

Following statistical analysis methods have been used : percentages, proportions, measures of central tendency, statistical significance tests namely, chi-square, t, z and F-Anova, and correlation coefficient.

LIMITATIONS OF THE STUDY

Limitation of the study are due to following reasons :

1. Due to Scope

The current level of quality management practices is intended to be explored only in selected manufacturing organisations. The service organisations have not been included even though quality of services is receiving increased attention now a days.

The geographical coverage of the present study is confined to Madhya Pradesh only. A wider coverage might have resulted in increased reliability of the findings.

2. *Due to Research Design*

The non probability sampling method had to be used. If adequate information were available, the probability sampling methods such as random sampling, could have been employed. Some managers were unwilling to participate in the study, it resulted in distortious in the research design. Some of the responses were partially filled up. It was accounted for, by adjusting the sample size on a question to question basis.

3. *Due to Personal Reasons*

The researcher is greatly handicapped by the non-availability of financial resources. Madhya Pradesh is the largest state of the country, in terms of area. Many industrial organisations are located in remote and far-flung areas. Therefore the researcher could not personally visit all the respondent organisations. As a result, the response to the questionnaire could not be supplemented with in-depth interviewing. .mb8

REFERENCES

Deming, W.E., 1986. Out of the Crisis, Cambridge Mass : MIT Press.

Emory, C.W. and Cooper, D.R., 1991. Business Research Methods, Homewood : Irwin.

Nunnally, J.C., 1981. Psychometric Theory, New Delhi : Tata McGraw Hill.

Saraph, J.V.; Banson, P.G.; Shroeder, R.G., 1989. "An Instrument for Measurings the Critical Factors of Quality Management". Decision Sciences, Vol. 20, No. 3, Summer, pp. 810 - 829.

Singh, A., 1991. "Total Quality Management : Concept and Practice in India". Productivity, Vol. 32, No. 3, October-December, pp. 393 - 399.

Sink, D.S., 1991. "TQM : The Nest Frontier or Just Another Bandwagon?". Productivity, Vol. 32, No. 3, October-December, pp. 400 - 414.

--, 1993. Industrial Compendium 1992, Bhopal : Directorate of Industries, Madhya Pradesh, p. 27. .pa

CHAPTER 4

QUALITY MANAGEMENT PRACTICES : INDEX AND MEASUREMENT

In this chapter the collected data has been analysed and interpreted in the light of objectives already stated. The hypotheses have been described at appropriate places.

The sample profile of the respondents and their organisations has been given. The respondents are classified on the basis of various parameters such as designation, age, educational qualification, work experience etc. Organisations are classified on the basis of single plant versus multi plant, type of production process, type of industry, age and size of the organisation, number of shifts operated etc. This analysis helps in developing a clearer picture of the respondents and their respective organisations, which leads to the development of a frame of reference for further analysis.

An instrument for measuring the Quality Management Practices has been developed for the specific purpose of this study. This instrument attempts to measure the level of quality management practices prevalent in the participating organisations, on the basis of opinions expressed by the quality manager of that organisation. A quality management practices index (QMPI) has also been developed.

The influence of characteristics such as size, and age of organisations; and type of the industries on quality management practices is studied. A number of hypotheses have been developed in this section which are tested for significance using the appropriate statistical tools.

SAMPLE PROFILE

On the basis of the information provided by the respondents, they and their respective organisations have been profiled in the following manner :

THE RESPONDENT'S PROFILE

The respondent's profile is given on the basis of responses received to the questions in part A of the questionnaire. The characteristics of participants are described in terms of following :

- Designation,
- Age,
- Educational Qualification,
- Work Experience,
- The Departments Represented.

DESIGNATION OF THE RESPONDENTS

Table 4.1 lists the designation of the respondents.

Table 4.1 Designation of Respondents

S.No.	Designation	Number of Respondents	Percentage
1.	Top Management (G.M./V.P./D.G.M./A.G.M., etc.)	5	10.63
2.	Works Manager (Divisional Manager, Plant Mgr.)	6	12.76
3.	Senior Manager and Manager	21	44.68
4.	Deputy Manager	7	14.89
5.	Engineer/Executive	8	17.04
	Total	47	

Top managements are from small single plant company, they considered quality management to be in their domain of activity. Works manager and deputy manager are from large multi plant company representing second to fourth level of management. Majority of the respondents (nearly 44%) are designated as managers/ senior managers.

AGE OF THE RESPONDENTS

In table 4.2 the age of the respondents is grouped into some classes and the frequency is mentioned against each class. The diagrammatic representation of data can be seen in fig.

Table 4.2 Frequency Distribution of Age of Respondents

S.No.	Age Years	Number of Respondents	Percentage
1.	21 - 25	6	12.76
2.	26 - 30	7	14.89
3.	31 - 35	8	17.02
4.	36 - 40	6	12.76
5.	41 - 45	12	25.55
6.	46 - 50	4	8.51
7.	Above 50	4	8.51
	Total	47	

Median age of respondents is 38 years and the range is from 23 to 56 years. Maximum of the respondents are in the age group of 41 to 45 years. It supports the finding given in table 4.1 as most of managers/senior managers are expected to be in the age group of 41 to 45 years.

EDUCATIONAL QUALIFICATIONS OF THE RESPONDENTS

The respondents have been classified on the basis of their educational background. The results are depicted in table 4.3.

Table 4.3 Educational Qualifications of Respondents

S.No.	Educational Qualification	Number of Respondents	Percentage
1.	Engineering:		
	a) Post Graduate	4	8.51
	b) Graduate	19	40.43
	c) Diploma	4	8.51
2.	Engineering with Management degree/diploma	6	12.76
3.	Non Engineering		
	a) P.G.	4	8.51
	b) Graduates	1	2.12

	c) Some other technical qualification	2	4.25
4.	Other Professional Qualification (MBA, CA, ICWA)	7	14.89
	Total	47	

Majority of the respondents (nearly 70%) are having Engineering background. This is understandable as quality/ production managers were approached for participating in this study. Persons having MBA or other professional qualifications such as CA, ICWA constitute nearly 15% of the sample. Remaining respondents are having non engineering and non professional educational background. There are 6 respondents who have both engineering and management qualification. They hail largely from younger age group.

WORK EXPERIENCE OF THE RESPONDENTS

The work experience (in years) of the respondents has been grouped into various classes. The results are given in table 4.4 and the diagrammatic representation is shown in fig. 4.2.

Table 4.4 Work Experience of Respondents - Frequency Distribution

S.No.	Experience - Years	Numberof Respondents	Percentage
1.	1 - 5	5	10.63
2.	6 - 10	14	29.78
3.	11 - 15	7	14.89
4.	16 - 20	8	17.02
5.	21 - 25	9	19.14
6.	Above 25	4	8.54
	Total	47	

Nearly 30% of the respondents have 6 to 10 years of work experience.

THE DEPARTMENTS REPRESENTED

The respondents were asked to mention the specific area of their work. On the basis of responses received, following table 4.5 has been prepared.

Table 4.5 Representation of various Departments in the Sample

S.No.	Departments	Number	Percentage
1.	Quality Control	33	42.30
2.	Production	20	25.64
3.	Production Planning & Control	14	17.95
4.	Product Development	6	7.69
5.	Process Development	4	5.14
6.	Research and Development	1	1.28
	Total	78	

Although the total number of respondents is 47 yet the total number of departments represented is coming out to be 78. It is due to the fact that many respondents claimed that their work is not confined to one department only. It is more evident in case of relatively smaller company where one person looks after several departments. Further this can also be attributed to the hierarchy of respondents. The higher is the hierarchy the larger number of departments they are expected to handle. Only one respondent claimed that he is looking after Research and Development Department. It is due to the fact that neglect of R & D activity is prevalent in most of the organisations. Those respondents who have mentioned Product and Process Development as their area of work have also claimed to work in other departments.

THE ORGANISATION'S PROFILE

Several questions were included in part B of the questionnaire which aimed at seeking information about the organisations. On the basis of information received the following characteristics of organisations are described :

(i) Multi plant or single plant
(ii) Applicability of ISO 9000 Series of Certification
(iii) Size of organisations
(iv) Age of organisations
(v) Type of industries
(vi) Type of production processes
(vii) Number of shifts operated.

Since the information regarding sales turnover and capacity of production is not provided by many of the respondents the same could not be taken as a base for categorisation of companies.

MULTI PLANT OR SINGLE PLANT

The participating companies have been classified on the basis of this information. Results are shown in table 4.6.

Table 4.6 Single Plant/Multiple-Plant organisations

S.No.	Type of organisation	Number	Percentage
1.	Single Plant	23	48.93%
2.	Multiple Plant	24	51.07%

Companies having multiple plants are marginally more than the single plant companies. The multi plant companies are relatively larger. This is to be expected as the large companies were intended to be included in the sample. Many of the multi plant companies have some of their plants outside Madhya Pradesh also.

APPLICABILITY OF ISO 9000 SERIES OF CERTIFICATION

The respondents were questioned about the applicability of ISO 9000 series of certification for their organisation. The results can be observed from table 4.7.

Table 4.7 Application of ISO 9000 Series of Certification

S.No.	ISO 9000 Series	Number of organisations	Percentage
1.	Applicable	23	48.93
2.	Non Applicable	24	51.07

Nearly 48% of the respondents affirmed that this certification is applicable for their organisation. These twenty three respondents were further questioned about the progress they have made for seeking this certification. The following table 4.8 describes the results (Fig. 4.3).

Table 4.8 Stage of ISO 9000 Certification

S.No.	Stage	Number of organisations	Percentage
1.	Initial	8	34.78
2.	Advanced	7	30.43
3.	Nearing Completion	5	21.73
4.	Certified	3	13.06
	Total	23	

As is clear from the above table nearly 34% of the organisations are in the initial stage of planning. While remaining 66% of the organisations are either in the advanced stage or have been given accreditation to one of the ISO 9000 series of certification. At the time of collection of data only three organisations in Madhya Pradesh were given this certification, namely Bharat Heavy Electrical Limited, Bhopal; Bhilai Steel Plant, Bhilai; and Kirloskar Brothers Limited, Dewas. All of them have been included in the sample. Afterwards another organisation namely Universal Cables Limited has also been certified. This organisation is not included in the sample.

SIZE OF ORGANISATIONS

The participating organisations have been classified on the basis of size of organisations. As has been stated in the preceding chapter, the criteria for this classification is number of employees in an organisation. Those organisations which are having 500 or more employees are considered as large organisations and those organisations which are having less than 500 employees are considered as small organisations. The results are shown in table 4.9

Table 4.9 Size Wise Distribution of Sample

Size	Number of Organisations	Percentage of Total
Large	21	44.68
Small	26	55.31
Total	47	

Small organisations are more in number than large organisations in the sample.

AGE OF ORGANISATIONS

Another criteria for classification of the participating organisation is the age of the organisation. The information about year of establishment of the company was gathered and it yielded the age of the organisation. Those companies which are ten years or more old are termed as the old organisations and companies which are in existence for less than 10 years are considered as new organisations. Results can be observed from table 4.10.

Table 4.10 Age Wise Distribution of Sample

Age	Number of Organisations	Percentage of Total
New	18	40.00
Old	27	60.00
Total	45	

The total number of organisations in this case are 45 as two companies did not divulge information about their year of establishment. Old organisations are more in number than new organisations.

TYPE OF INDUSTRIES

The organisations have been classified on the basis of type of industries. Five categories have been made, viz. Engineering, Pharmaceutical and Chemical, Electrical and Electronics, Agrobased, and Textiles Industries. Table 4.11 gives the detailed results.

Table 4.11 Type Wise Distribution of Sample

S.No.	Type	Number of Organisations	Percentage of Total
1.	Engineering	18	38.29
2.	Pharmaceuticals and Chemicals	11	23.40
3.	Electrical and Electronics	8	17.02
4.	Agrobased	5	10.63
5.	Textile	5	10.63
	Total	47	

Majority of the organisations are from the engineering industry. All the three organisations which have been awarded ISO 9000 certification are engineering organisations. This finding is in agreement with that of Gandhi (1993). Pharmaceutical and Chemical industries have been merged due to similarities in the production process. Since Madhya Pradesh ranks second in the country in the production of oil seeds, agrobased companies have also been included in the sample. Soya plants are predominant in this type of industry.

TYPE OF PRODUCTION PROCESSES

The distribution of the sample has been done on the basis of type of production processes. The results are depicted in table 4.12 given below.

Table 4.12 Types of Production Processes

S.No.	Stage	Number of organisations	Percentage
a.	Job order	7	14.89
b.	Batch production	10	21.27
c.	Continuous production	25	53.21

d.	**Assembly line**	3	6.38
e.	**Continuous-cum-Assembly**	2	4.25
	Total	**47**	

The highest number of companies are in 'continuous' type. It is understandable also as all the steel, chemical, and soya plant are continuous process type. Next in order is the batch production type which is the process used in pharmaceutical companies. There are only two organisations in the continuous-cum-assembly category.

NUMBER OF SHIFTS OPERATED

The distribution of companies on the basis of 'number of shifts operated' is mentioned in table 4.13.

Table 4.13 Number of Shifts Run by the Company

No. of Shifts	Number of organisations	Percentage
One	4	8.5
Two	6	12.76
Three	37	78.72
Total	47	

Seventy eight percent of the companies operate three shifts. It supports the finding that majority of the companies are having continuous type of production process. Some companies do not have continuous process but operate on three shift basis.

QUALITY MANAGEMENT PRACTICES INDEX

As has been highlighted in the review of literature that many authorities on the subject of Quality Management are placing increased emphasis on studying Quality Management Practices prevalent in an organisation. Many of these practices are applicable over a cross section of industries. The development and propagation of international standards such as ISO 9000 series of certification, Malcom bridge awards, and Quality Management Bench mark Assessment (QMBA) are basically aimed at assessment certification of prevalent practices and documentation procedure.

In the preceding chapter the development of an instrument to be used for this study has been described. It lists the practices relevant to the Quality Management. Thirty seven statements have been included in this instrument. The respondents were asked to rate their organisation's practices on a six point interval rating scale. With its help a quantitative measure termed as Quality Management Practices Index (QMPI) has been calculated. The QMPI has been considered as a criteria for classification of companies in forthcoming sections of this chapter.

CALCULATION OF QUALITY MANAGEMENT PRACTICES INDEX

For the purpose of developing the Quality Management Practices Index, the following eight factors were identified :

1. Role of Management
2. Role of Quality Department
3. Training of Employees
4. Product Design
5. Supplier Quality Management
6. Inspection
7. Quality Data
8. Employee Relations

The instrument contained 37 statements which comprehensively cover facets of these factors which in turn cover Quality Management Practices. To quantify the response a six point scale has been used. Each statement was given a score ranging from 0 to 5. The cumulated score of the respondent has been used as Quality Management Practices Index for each company. The range for QMPI is from zero to one hundred eighty five. All the QMPI values have been arranged in ascending order using the data array method. One of the measures of central tendency, median is taken as a cut-off point to divide the 47 companies into two categories. Median value for these

47 ungrouped observations comes to be 137. The companies whose QMPI value was less than 137 were classified in low QMPI companies while the companies with QMPI value of 137 or more were put in high QMPI companies category.

The Quality Management Practices Score (QMPS) of all the companies have been arranged in the form of frequency distribution. The results are shown in table 4.14.

4.14 Frequency Distribution of QMP Score (QMPS)

S.No.	QMP Score	Number of Organisations	Percentage of Total
1.	41 - 60	2	04.25
2.	61 - 80	1	02.12
3.	81 - 100	6	12.76
4.	101 - 120	7	14.89
5.	121 - 140	12	25.53
6.	141 - 160	13	27.65
7.	161 - 180	6	12.76
	Total	47	

Analysis of the above data reveals that more than 50% of the total respondents fall in the range of 121 to 160 score value of Quality Management Practices.

To determine whether the low categories actually differ with respect to QMPI, test for significance of means has been performed. The results are depicted in table 4.15.

Table 4.15 Test for Difference of Means between two categories of QMPI.

	High Category	Low Category
Mean	$\overline{X}_H = 152.92$	$\overline{X}_L = 104.48$
Sample Variance	$S_1^2 = 2496.44$	$S_2^2 = 506.68$
Sample Size	$n_1 = 24$	$n_2 = 23$

$$t = \frac{\overline{X}_H - \overline{X}_L}{(S_1^2/n_1 + S_2^2/n_2)}$$

t = 4.29

d.f. = $n_1 + n_2 - 1 = 46$

Normal value is used.

't' value is significant at 5% level.

As is clear from the above table the two categories differ significantly at 95% level of confidence. It means that the categorisation of companies on the basis of QMPI values in two categories of high and low QMPI is justified.

VALIDATION OF QUALITY MANAGEMENT PRACTICES INDEX

A question (No. 22, Part D), was inserted to check the internal consistency of the respondent's attitude towards his perception of quality factors discussed earlier, and overall effectiveness of quality department. A five point Likert type scale was used to develop a quantitative measure for the responses. It is expected that companies with low QMPI will have a low score for this question and vice versa. The test for significance of coefficient of correlation has been applied. The results can be observed from table 4.16.

Table 4.16 Relationship between QMPI and Quality Department's Effectiveness.

Factor	Value of 'r'	Test statistics value	Remarks
QMP and Quality Departments Effectiveness	0.56	4.43	Significant at 5% level

It is concluded that the two aspects correlate positively and this correlation is significant at 5% level of significance, as the calculated value of 't' 4.43 is much higher than the table value of 1.96. The positive correlation between these two aspects indicates a little towards the QMPI instrument's validity. But conclusively from this single test, validity of the instrument can not be claim in absolute terms.

INDIVIDUAL STATEMENTS ANALYSIS AND RANKING OF FACTORS OF QUALITY MANAGEMENT PRACTICES

The instrument contains thirty seven statements which cover the Quality Management Practices of a company. The mean scores for each of the statement has been calculated by analysing the 47 responses for each statement and taking the average of the ratings given by the respondents. The results have been arranged according to the ranks and are depicted in table 4.17.

Table 4.17 Mean Scores of Measures of Quality Management

S.No.	Quality Control Measures	Mean Score	Ranks
1.	Responsibility for quality control programme	4.23	1
2.	Specificity of Quality goals	4.17	2
3.	Visibility of Quality Department	4.04	3
4.	Access to the top management	4.04	3
5.	Availability of quality data	4.02	4
6.	Importance of Quality	4.00	5
7.	Autonomy	3.93	6
8.	Effectiveness of the Quality department	3.85	7
9.	Coordination	3.82	8
10.	Traceability	3.82	8
11.	Use of quality data as a tool to manage quality	3.82	8
12.	Efforts to develop Quality policy	3.80	9
13.	Clarity of product specifications	3.76	10
14.	Importance of Inspection review	3.72	11
15.	Timeliness of quality data	3.53	12
16.	Selection of suppliers based on Quality	3.40	13
17.	Product development process	3.38	14
18.	Resources for employee training	3.36	15
19.	Understanding of Quality policy	3.34	16
20.	Producibility	3.31	17
21.	Throughness of supplier rating system	3.29	18
22.	Recognition of employee's Quality performance	3.27	19

23.	Process design	3.25	20
24.	Preventive equipment maintenance	3.23	21
25.	Thoroughness of product design	3.23	21
26.	Training for basic statistical techniques	3.17	22
27.	Training	3.12	23
28.	Reliance on few dependable suppliers	3.06	24
29.	Effectiveness of training	2.91	25
30.	Use of acceptance sampling	2.80	26
31.	Advanced Training	2.78	27
32.	Display of quality related information	2.76	28
33.	Use of statistical control charts	2.51	29
34.	Employee involvement programs	2.44	30
35.	Participation of workers in Quality decisions	2.38	31
36.	Frequency of design changes	2.38	31
37.	Effectiveness of employee involvement programs	2.36	32

The highest possible mean score for each statement is 5. It can be observed from the table that nearly 40% of the statements have a mean score hovering around 4. It means that the Quality Management Practices denoted by these statements are being practiced at 'high' level.

As is clear from the above table that practices such as employee involement type programmes and frequency of design changes are given less attention by the management. Further application of statistical control charts and dissemination of quality information is also not being given enough attention. Training of workers is considered relatively unimportant. The provision of advanced training for workers is given even less priority. This might be due to the fact that management does not consider Human Resource Development aspects seriously. Due to inadequate resources and shortage of manpower the management finds it difficult to takeup developmental efforts like training of its employees. The effectiveness of training programs is also rated very low by the respondents as training is provided in haphazard manner.

Practices regarding product design are not being given proper attention. On the other hand the design changes should be more frequent, according to the recent trend and changing needs. It is clear that employee relations are given the least priority while it is essential for the success of Quality Management. This finding is in contradiction with that of Singh (1991). Practices like quality circles, quality improvement teams or the employee involvement type programes should be taken up to ensure increased participation of workers in quality control.

The factor wise ranking has also been attempted by taking the average of mean scores for all the statements pertaining to that factor. The ranking is assigned to factors on the basis of this score. The results can be observed from table 4.18.

Table 4.18 Ranking of Factors of Quality Management

S.No.	Factors	Average Mean	Rank Score
1.	Role of Quality Department	3.93	I
2.	Role of Management	3.90	II
3.	Quality Data	3.53	III
4.	Product Design	3.31	IV
5.	Supplier Quality Management	3.25	V
6.	Inspection	3.10	VI
7.	Training of Employees	3.06	VII
8.	Employee Relations	2.61	VIII

Majority of the factors (87.5%) have average mean scores above 3 which indicates the level of aggregate Quality Management Practices in the participating companies is above average.

The practices which constitute Role of Quality Department & Role of Management are being pursued at a very high level by the sample organisations. In quality manager's opinion the Quality Department has been given sufficient autonomy, access and importance by the top management. Similarly the top management in the population takes up responsibility for Quality Control, specificity of Quality Goals and Development of Quality Policy. However, the understanding of Quality Policy by lower rungs of hierarchy is not reported to be high. This is due to less involvement of employees in Quality related issue. The success of Quality Management requires total commitment by all the employees of the organisation. The factor employee relation is ranked as the last which indicates that enough attention is not being paid to boost employee morale and to motivate them to contribute towards quality improvement.

MEASUREMENT OF QUALITY MANAGEMENT PRACTICES

For the purpose of analysis the response to the instrument has been quantified by using the procedure which has been described earlier. It was felt that the Organisation's characteristics such as size and age will influence the Quality Management Practices.

SIZE WISE ANALYSIS (AGGREGATE & FACTOR WISE)

The classification of organisations on the basis of size has already been discussed earlier. For analysing the influence of size of organisations on Quality Management Practices (both aggregate & factor wise), following nine null hypotheses have been formulated :

$H_0 1$: There is no significant difference between the large sized and the small sized organisations with regards to "aggregate quality management practices." $H_0 2$: With regards to "Role of Management" the large sized & the small sized organisations do not differ significantly.

$H_0 3$: With regards to "Role of Quality Department" there is no significant difference between the small sized and the large sized organisations.

$H_0 4$: There is no significant difference between the large sized and the small sized organisations with regards to "training of employees."

$H_0 5$: With regards to "Product design" there is no significant difference between the large sized and small sized organisations.

$H_0 6$: With regards to "Supplier Quality Management" the large sized and the small sized organisations do not differ significantly.

$H_0 7$: The large sized and the small sized organisations do not differ significantly with regards to "Inspection".

$H_0 8$: With regards to "Quality data" there is no significant difference between the small sized and the large sized organisations. .mb6

$H_0 9$: There is no significant difference between the large sized and the small sized organisations with regards to "Employee relations"

The above hypotheses seek to establish that large and small size organisations differ with respect to the aggregate Quality Management Practices as well as factor wise Quality Management Practices. These hypotheses were tested by using the test of difference of means at 5% level of significance with degrees of freedom 45. The critical value has been taken from normal table, which is 1.96 at 5% level of significance. Summarised results are presented in table 4.19.

Table 4.19 Tests for Difference of Means between Large & Small Size Organisations

Null Hypotheses	Calculated Z Value	Result
$H_0 1$	1.209	Accepted
$H_0 2$	0.147	Accepted
$H_0 3$	1.13	Accepted
$H_0 4$	3.72	**Rejected**
$H_0 5$	1.98	**Rejected**
$H_0 6$	0.232	Accepted
$H_0 7$	0.794	Accepted
$H_0 8$	1.99	**Rejected**
$H_0 9$	0.112	Accepted

A quick look at the above table would reveal that all null hypotheses except $H_0 4$, $H_0 5$ and $H_0 8$ have been accepted. In other words there is statistical evidence available to believe that the large and small size organisations differ significantly with respect to the following factors of Quality Management Practices :

- Training of Employees

- Product Design
- Quality Data

The level of practices reported by large organisations are relatively of higher level with respect to the above three factors. One possible explanation may be that adequate resources are available for training of employees in large organisations. Here the scale of production is large, number of products in the product mix are more, and product development and product diversification activities are taken up which result in increased attention being given to training of employees, frequent changes in product design, and generation of quality data. Further, employees of the large organisation are more likely to be given advanced training then their counterparts in the smaller organisations. Difference among the above factors is not large enough, that is why the aggregate Quality Management Practices scores of large and small size organisations do not differ significantly

AGE WISE ANALYSIS (AGGREGATE & FACTOR WISE)

The respondent organisations have been classified on the basis of age of the organisation. For analysing the influence of age of organisations on Quality Management Practices (both aggregate & factor wise), following nine null hypotheses have been formulated :

$H_0$10 : The old and the new companies do not differ significantly with regards to "Aggregate Quality Management Practices".

$H_0$11 : With regards to "Role of Management" the old and the new companies do not differ significantly.

$H_0$12 : With regards to "Role of Quality Department" there is no significant difference between the old and the new companies.

$H_0$13 : The old and the new companies do not differ significantly with regards to "training of employees".

$H_0$14 : With regards to "Product design" there is no significant difference between the old and the new companies.

$H_0$15 : With regards to "Supplier Quality Management" the old and the new companies do not differ significantly.

$H_0$16 : The old and the new companies do not differ significantly with regards to "Inspection"

$H_0$17 : With regards to "Quality data" there is no significant difference between the old and the new companies.

$H_0$18 : There is no significant difference between the old and the new companies with regards to "Employee relations"

The above hypotheses seek to establish through statistical tools that new and old organisation differ with respect to the aggregate and factor wise Quality Management Practices. The summarised result of hypotheses testing are depicted in table 4.20.

Table 4.20 Tests for Difference of Means between New & Old Organisations

Null Hypotheses	Calculated Z Value	Result
$H_0$10	0.851	Accepted
$H_0$11	1.14	Accepted
$H_0$12	0.648	Accepted
$H_0$13	0.98	Accepted
$H_0$14	2.04	**Rejected**
$H_0$15	1.05	Accepted
$H_0$16	0.07	Accepted
$H_0$17	1.20	Accepted
$H_0$18	0.40	Accepted

As is clear from the above table only null hypothesis $H_0$14 is rejected and all others have been accepted. It means there is statistical evidence available to believe that the old and new organisations differ with respect to product design only.

In old organisations the production activity has been streamlined and a resistance to change has developed, which is probably why product design activities are given less attention. This explains the significant different between new and old organisations with regards to product design. The old and new organisations do not differ significantly with respect to training of employees. It is hard to explain because it was expected that training of employees is required more in new organisations. Many new organisations are results of foreign collaborations, wherein sufficient resources are earmarked for training. Similarly new organisations were expected to perform better inspection related practices. As their measuring instruments are more advanced and sophisticated the generation of quality data will be comparatively more. Effects of technological changes are likely to affect more new organisations than old organisations. As results of tests of significance indicate that all these hypotheses have been rejected.

For factors of quality management practices such as role of management, role of quality department, inspection, supplier's quality management, and employee relations both the company characteristics size and age do not differ significantly among themselves.

DEPENDENCE OF SIZE & AGE OF ORGANISATION ON LOW AND HIGH LEVELS OF QUALITY MANAGEMENT PRACTICES

Companies have been classified on the basis of low and high levels of Quality Management Practices. The following hypotheses were formulated to test whether the company characteristics are dependent on the level of Quality Management Practices.

$H_0$19 : Size of the organisation is independent of the level of Quality Management Practices.

$H_0$20 : Age of the organisation is independent of the level of Quality Management Practices.

Table 4.21 Dependence of Size and Age of Organisations on Levels of Quality Management Practices

Null Hypotheses	Chi-Square Calculated Value	Value Table Value At 5%	Result
$H_0 19$	4.994	3.841	Rejected
$H_0 20$	0.133	3.841	Accepted

The above two hypotheses were tested using chi-square analysis at 5% level of significance.

The first null hypothesis that "size of the organisation is independent of the quality management practices", is rejected. Therefore it is concluded that size of the organisation and quality management practices are dependent on each other.

The second null hypothesis was accepted. i.e. age of the organisation is independent of the quality management practices prevalent in that organisation.

The size of the organisation influences the level of Quality Management Practices Index more than age of organisations. The level of Quality Management Practice in large organisations are expected to be of higher level because the number of employees are more, market size is bigger, level of competition is high. On the other hand age of organisation is not dependent on the level of Q.M.P.I. It may possibly be due to the fact that new organisations might be facing initial production hassles to devote sufficient time to Quality Management related issues.

RELATIONSHIPS BETWEEN ORGANISATIONAL CHARACTERISTICS AND QUALITY MANAGEMENT PRACTICES

For the purpose of exploring relationship between size and age of organisations and the Quality Management Practices, following two null hypotheses have been formulated.

$H_0 21$: There is no relationship between size of organisations and Quality Management Practices.

$H_0$22 : There is no relationship between age of organisations and Quality Management Practices.

For testing the above two hypotheses, two correlation coefficients have been calculated between the number of employees in an organisation and its Quality Management Practices Score; and between age in years of an organisation and its Quality Management Practices Score. Tests of significance for 'r' have been performed to see whether the correlations are significant. The results are summarised in table 4.22

Table 4.22 Correlation between Size & QMP, and Age & QMP

Factor Combination	Value of r	Test Statistics Value	Remarks
1. Size and QMP	0.528	4.17	Significant
2. Age and QMP	0.094	0.63	Not Significant

It is of interest to note that although both the correlations are positive only the correlation between size and QMP was found to be significant at 5% level of significance with 45 degrees of freedom, i.e. $H_0$21 is rejected.

RELATIONSHIP BETWEEN TYPE OF INDUSTRIES & QUALITY MANAGEMENT PRACTICES (AGGREGATE & FACTOR WISE)

For the purpose of this study 5 types of industries have been considered namely, Engineering, Pharmaceuticals and Chemicals, Electricals and Electronics, Agrobased, and Textiles.

For the purpose of analysis following nine null hypotheses have been formulated :

$H_0$23 : There is no difference among types of industries with respect to 'Aggregate Quality Management Practices'.

$H_0$24 : There is no difference among types of industries with respect to 'Role of Management'

$H_0$25 : There is no difference among types of industries with respect to 'Role of Quality Department'.

$H_0$26 : There is no difference among types of industries with respect to 'Training of Employees'.

$H_0$27 : There is no difference among types of industries with respect to 'Product Design'.

$H_0$28 : There is no difference among types of industries with respect to 'Supplier Quality Management'

$H_0$29 : There is no difference among types of industries with respect to 'Inspection'.

$H_0$30 : There is no difference among types of industries with respect to 'Quality Data'.

$H_0$31 : There is no difference among types of industries with respect to 'Employee Relations'

The above hypotheses seek to find out whether the types of industries have an effect on both the aggregate and factor wise Quality Management Practices. F-ANOVA test for one way classification has been applied for testing above hypotheses. Thus nine ANOVA tests have been performed. The results are mentioned in table 4.23.

Table 4.23Summarised results of F-ANOVA test-difference among Types of Industries and Quality Management Practices

S.No.	Description	F-value	Remarks
1.	Aggregate Quality Management Practices Significant	0.33	Not
2.	Role of Management	0.54	"
3.	Role of Quality Department	0.17	"
4.	Training of Employees	0.38	"
5.	Product Design	0.34	"
6.	Supplier Quality Management	0.59	"
7.	Inspection	0.85	"
8.	Quality Data	0.34	"
9.	Employee Relations	1.03	"

Source : Appendix F.

As is clear from the above table that the hypotheses $H_0$23 to $H_0$31 stand accepted i.e. the types of industries do not differ among themselves for both aggregate and factor wise Quality Management Practices.

The above results indicate that the different type of industries do not influence the Quality Management Practices in the population. One possible explanation is that the design of these Quality Management Practices factors are not intended to be industry specific. Some variation were observed in the level of Q.M.P. scores of Engineering industries & Agrobased industries, farmer being higher; but the difference is not large enough.

REFERENCES

Gandhi, R.S., 1993. ''ISO-9000-Challenges to the Textile Industry''. New Cloth Market, Aug., pp. 8 - 10.

Singh, A., 1991. ''Total Quality Management : Concept and Practice in India''. Productivity, Vol. 32, No.3, October-December.

CHAPTER 5

QUALITY MANAGEMENT PRACTICES IMPACT OF ORGANISATIONAL ENVIRONMENT

Through rigorous search of literature following five environmental factors prevailing in manufacturing organisations have been identified.

1. Quality Manager's Access to the Top Management
2. Frequency of Production Stoppage Due to Non-Conformance
3. Organisation's Response to Stoppage in Production
4. Facilitating Environment for Quality Management
5. Inspection Related Practices

In this chapter an attempt has been made to study these environmental factors with respect to size and age of organisations; and also with respect to type of industries.

QUALITY MANAGER'S ACCESS TO THE TOP MANAGEMENT SIZE WISE

The information was sought on Quality Manager's line relationships with his superiors. The intent was to determine Quality Manager's access to the top management. The size wise responses on this aspect are mentioned in table 5.1.

Table 5.1 Quality Manager's Access To The Top Management : Size Wise

S. No.	Quality Manager Reporting To	Large Size (Total No.=21)		Small Size (Total No.=26)	
		Number of Organisations	% of Total	Number of Organisations	% of Total
1.	Top Management	13	61.90	19	73.07
2.	Works Manager	4	19.04	5	19.23
3.	Production Manager	2	09.52	1	03.84
4.	Any Other	2	09.52	1	03.84

As is clear from the above table that majority of the respondents in both large (61.9%) and small (73.07%) size organisations report to the top management. In both large and small organisations approximately 19% of the respondents report to the Works Manager. It is interesting to note that in large size organisations comparatively more respondents report to the Production Manager, than in small size organisations. Two respondents in large size category and one respondent in small size category have not specified the designation of their superior but marked their response under 'Any Other' category.

It is evident from the above table that in large size organisations nearly 38% of the respondents are reporting to the managers other than top management. While in small size organisations relatively more number of respondents are reporting to the top management. This might be due to the fact that in small size organisations there are less hierarchical line relationships.

Age Wise The results of age wise classification of this aspect are given below in Table 5.2.

Table 5.2 Quality Manager's Access To The Top Management : Age Wise

S. No.	Quality Manager Reporting To	New Companies (Total No.=18)		Old Companies (Total No.=27)	
		Number of Organisations	% of Total	Number of Organisations	% of Total
1.	Top Management	11	66.11	20	74.07
2.	Works Manager	3	16.66	6	22.22
3.	Production Manager	2	11.11	0	0.0
4.	Any Other	2	11.11	1	3.70

A quick look at the above table would reveal that majority of the respondents in both new (66%) and old (74%) report to the top management. Sixteen percent of the respondents in new organisations report to the works manager, while the same figure for old organisations is 22%. Two respondents in new organisations report to the Production Manager. None of the respondents in old organisations report to the Production Manager. In one of the two responses where the information about year of establishment was not given, rendering them unusable for age wise analysis, the quality manager was reporting to the production manager. It explains variation in this figure with respect to size wise and age wise category. It is clear from the above table that comparatively more number of respondents report to the top management in old organisations. It might be due to the fact that the production in old organisations would have been streamlined which may result in easy access to the top management. In new organisations it is expected that organisational structure may be evolving which results in more than 20% of the respondents reporting either to the Production Manager or to the Manager whose designation has not been specified.

TYPE WISE

As has been stated earlier, five types of industries have been considered for this study. Table 5.3 gives the industry wise

Table 5.3 Quality Manager's Access to the Top Management : Type wise

S. No.	Quality Manager Reporting To	Type I* Total-18		Type II* Total-11		Type III* Total-08		Type IV* Total-05		Type V* Total-05	
		No.	%	No.	%	No.	%	No.	%	No.	%
1.	Top Management	16	88.88	8	72.72	5	62.5	1	20.0	2	40.0
2.	Works Manager	2	11.12	1	9.09	2	25.0	2	40.0	2	40.0
3.	Production Manager	—	—	2	18.19	1	12.5	—	—	—	—
4.	Any Other	—	—	—	—	—	—	2	40.0	1	20.0

Type I = Engineering,
Type II = Pharmaceutical & Chemical,
Type III = Electrical & Electronics,
Type IV = Agrobased,
Type V = Textiles

information on Quality Manager's access to the top management. (Pls. see table on the next page)

The results indicate that maximum number of the respondents in Engineering industry, i.e., nearly 89%, report to the top management followed by nearly 73% in pharmaceuticals & chemicals industry. Respectively 18% and 12% respondents report to the Production Manager in pharmaceuticals & chemicals, and electricals & electronics industry.

It is obvious from the above results that except in Agro-based industry, in all other types of industries, majority of the respondents have direct and easy access to the top management by virtue of their reporting relationships. It is to be expected as in general, Quality Management Practices in engineering and pharmaceutical industries, are relatively of higher level.

It is clear from findings of the study that nearly 60% to 70% Quality Managers are reporting to the top management. It is in support of the findings of Groocock (1974), and Raju (1987). According to them the cardinal principle is that the Quality Manager should report to the top management and not to the Production Manager, so that it is free of control by those whom it is measuring.

FREQUENCY OF PRODUCTION STOPPAGE DUE TO NON-CONFORMANCE

Size Wise

The information was obtained from the frequency of interruptions in production as a result of product's non-conformance to the specifications. Size-wise results are depicted below in table 5.4.

Table 5.4 Frequency Of Production Stoppage Due To Non-Conformance : Size Wise

S. No.	Frequency	Large Size (Total No.=21)		Small Size (Total No.=26)	
		Number of Organisations	% of Total	Number of Organisations	% of Total
1.	Never	4	19.04	8	30.76
2.	Less Frequently	17	80.95	16	61.53
3.	Frequently	0	0.0	2	07.69
4.	More Frequently	0	0.0	0	0.0

Majority of the respondents in large (80%) and small (61%) report that interruptions in production due to non-conformance are less frequent. In large organisations the remaining organisations report that production is never stopped due to this reason. Nearly 7% of the small organisations report that production is frequently stopped. In the same category 31% of the respondents claim that production is never stopped due to non-conformance. It might be due to the fact that relatively smaller organisations may not have formal Quality Management System, resulting in less stringent check on the quality of products.

Age Wise

Table 5.5 lists the results of age-wise classification on this aspect.

Table 5.5 Frequency Of Production Stoppage Due To Non-Conformance : Age Wise

S. No.	Frequency	New Companies (Total No.=18)		Old Companies (Total No.=27)	
		Number of Organisations	% of Total	Number of Organisations	% of Total
1.	Never	3	16.66	9	33.33
2.	Less Frequently	14	77.77	17	62.96
3.	Frequently	1	5.55	1	3.7
4.	More Frequently	0	0.0	0	0.0

Majority of respondents in new (78%) and old (63%) organisations report that interruption in production due to non-conformance are less frequent. None of the respondents in both the categories have marked the response 'More Frequently'. One third of the old organisations report that production is never stopped due to non-conformance. It might be due to the fact that in old companies the production has become stream lined and initial production hassles such as design problems have been overcome. It explains the relatively more number of 'Never Responses' in this category.

Type Wise

Table 5.6 given below, shows results of variations due to types of industries for this particular aspect. (Pls. see table on the next page).

Except in Engineering industry in which 11% of the organisations report frequent stoppage in production, respondents in all other industries have mentioned either less frequency or no interruptions in production. For Textiles industry majority of the organisations report that production is never stopped. It is followed by engineering industry.

As is clear from the above analysis, majority of the respondents have reported that production is either never stopped or less frequently stopped due to non-conformance. For 'never' responses, it is not clear whether production is never stopped because product conforms to the specifications every time, or non-conformance is overlooked and production is allowed to be continued even though some non-conforming products are being produced. The possibility of later case is high. It reflects the attitude an organisation towards quality.

ORGANISATION'S RESPONSE TO STOPPAGE IN PRODUCTION

For the purpose of analysis of this item of information, those respondents have been excluded who have marked 'NeverResponse' in the preceding sub-section. Three questions

Table 5.6 Quality Manager's Access to the Top Management : Type wise

S. No.	Frequency	Type I* Total-18		Type II* Total-11		Type III* Total-08		Type IV* Total-05		Type V* Total-05	
		No.	%	No.	%	No.	%	No.	%	No.	%
1.	Never	5	27.77	2	18.18	2	25.0	1	20.0	2	40.0
2.	Less Frequently	11	61.11	9	81.82	6	75.0	4	80.0	3	60.0
3.	Frequently	2	11.12	—	—	—	—	—	—	—	—
4.	More Frequently	—	—	—	—	—	—	—	—	—	—

Type I = Engineering,
Type II = Pharmaceutical & Chemical,
Type III = Electrical & Electronics,
Type IV = Agrobased,
Type V = Textiles

have been inserted which seek response on a dichotomous type 'Yes/No' scale. Only those respondents who have given the response in affirmative, their number have been mentioned against each item of information.

Size Wise

The results of organisation's response to stoppage in production with reference to size of the organisations are mentioned in table 5.7

Table 5.7 Organisation's Response To Stoppage In Production : Size Wise

S. No.	Response	Large Size Total No.=21-Never=17		Small Size Total No.=26-Never=18	
		Number of Organisations	% of Total	Number of Organisations	% of Total
1.	Immediate Action	16	94.11	17	94.44
2.	Availability of Trouble Shooting List	4	3.52	9	50.00
3.	Documentation of Lost Time	2	11.76	3	16.66

Nearly 94% of the organisations in both the categories have given the affirmative response to 'Immediate Action' in the wake of stoppage in production. 50% of the small organisations report that trouble shooting list is available to handle the situation resulting from production stoppage. The same figure in large organisations is relatively less. In both the categories very less number of respondents have answered in affirmative to the practice of 'Documentation of Lost Time'. The higher number of organisations in small size organisations reporting availability of trouble shooting list is hard to explain. It might be due to the fact that in small organisations less number of production lines might be operating, therefore, the management in these organisations must be eager to restart the production soon. It possibly explains relatively high number of respondents in this category reporting in affirmative to the practice of documentation of lost time.

Age Wise

Table 5.8 depicts the results of this aspect with respect to the age of organisation.

Table 5.8 Organisation's Response To Stoppage In Production : Age Wise

S. No.	Response	New Companies Total No.= 15		Old Companies Total No.= 18	
		Number of Organisations	% of Total	Number of Organisations	% of Total
1.	Immediate Action	15	100.00	16	88.88
2.	Availability of Trouble Shooting List	09	60.00	04	22.22
3.	Documentation of Lost Time	02	13.33	03	16.66

As is clear from the above table, newer organisations are reporting comparatively better level of practices which is evinced by the fact that all the respondents in new organisations have answered in affirmative to the 'Immediate Action' response. Similarly, more number of respondents (60%), in new organisation's category, report that trouble shooting list is readily available. It is in contrast to only 22% of respondents in old organisation's category. This might be due to the fact that the Quality Management team in old organisations may have become so accustomed to handling such situations that they do not require help of trouble shooting list.

Type Wise

Table 5.9 presents type-wise results of organisation's response to stoppage in production. (Pls. see table on the next page)

Table 5.9 Quality Manager's Access to the Top Management : Type wise

S. No. Response	Type I* Total-13		Type II* Total-09		Type III* Total-06		Type IV* Total-04		Type V* Total-03	
	No.	%	No.	%	No.	%	No.	%	No.	%
1. Immediate Action	12	92.30	8	88.88	6	100.00	4	100.0	3	100.0
2. Availability of Trouble Shooting list	6	46.15	3	33.33	2	33.33	2	50.0	—	—
3. Documentation of Lost Time	2	15.38	2	22.22	—	—	1	25.0	—	—

Type I = Engineering,
Type II = Pharmaceutical & Chemical,
Type III = Electrical & Electronics,
Type IV = Agrobased,
Type V = Textiles

All the respondents in three types of industries, viz, Electricals & Electronics, Agro-based, and Textiles industry have answered in affirmative that immediate action is taken to restart the production process. No organisation in Electrical & Electronics, and Textiles industries have answered in affirmative to the practice of documentation of last time. The down-time analysis is receiving more importance in Pharmaceuticals and Chemicals, as well as Engineering industry.

To sum up, most of the organisations claim that immediate action is taken so that production is restarted. Practices like availability of trouble shooting list is receiving relatively less attention of Quality Managers. It is difficult to understand without trouble shooting list what sort of immediate action is being taken. The practice of documentation of lost time is given the least attention, which otherwise might have resulted in idle time analysis and other related aspects of capacity utilisation and productivity measurement.

FACILITATING ENVIRONMENT FOR QUALITY MANAGEMENT

Some factors have been identified which contribute towards facilitating the environment for Quality Managements. These factors are policy based and have long term implications. For the purpose of analysis, four questions have been included to seek response on a 'Yes/No' type dichotomous scale. Only those respondents have been counted whose answers were in affirmative to the presence of facilititating environmental factors in their organisations.

Size Wise

Results of effect of size of organisations on these facilitating environmental factors are depicted in table 5.10.

Table 5.10 Facilitating Environment For Quality Management : Size Wise

S. No.	Factors	Large Size (Total No.=21)		Small Size (Total No.=26)	
		Number of Organisation	% of Total	Number of Organisation	% of Total
1.	Issuance of "Product" Brief By Marketing Department	19	90.47	24	92.30
2.	Existence of Customer Complaint System	19	90.47	19	73.07
3.	Availability of Written And Approved Procedure For Sampling	19	90.47	26	100.00
4.	Internal Laboratory Facilities	21	100.00	24	92.30

It is evident from the above results that all the factors have been reported to be present by respondents hailing from both large and small organisations. Only, in small organisations relatively less number of respondents reported that the customer complaint system exists in their organisations. This is understandable as small organisations have less resources to spend on such systems. Secondly, they have relatively smaller market therefore they may rely on some informal system for redressal of customer's grievances.

Age Wise

The table 5.11 gives the information with respect to age group categories.

Table 5.11 Facilitating Environment For Quality Management : Age wise

S. No.	Factors	New Companies (Total No.=18)		Old Companies (Total No.=27)	
		Number of Organisations	% of Total	Number of Organisations	% of Total
1.	Issuance of "Product" Brief By Marketing Department	16	88.88	26	96.29
2.	Existence of Customer Complaint System	15	83.33	22	81.48
3.	Availability of Written And Approved Procedure For Sampling	16	88.88	27	100.00
4.	Internal Laboratory Facilities	17	94.44	26	96.29

The results show that more old organisations report presence of facilitating environmental factors as compared to new organisations, especially for the factors of 'Sampling Procedure' and 'Product Brief'. For the other two factors both new and old organisations report the same levels of practice.

Type Wise

The effects of types of industries on the presence or absence of facilitating environmental factors have been studied and the results are mentioned in table 5.12. (Pls. see table on the next page)

Relatively less number of organisations in Agro-based industry report the presence of all the four factors. However both Engineering and Electricals & Electronics industry report better presence of all these factors. This might be due to the fact that Quality Manager's in Soya plant devote less time to customer's satisfaction.

Presence of nearly all of facilitating environmental factors have been reported by the respondents. The existence of

Table 5.12 Facilitating Environment For Quality Management : Type Wise

S. No.	Factors	Type I Total-18 No.	Type I Total-18 %	Type II Total-11 No.	Type II Total-11 %	Type III Total-08 No.	Type III Total-08 %	Type IV Total-05 No.	Type IV Total-05 %	Type V Total-05 No.	Type V Total-05 %
1.	Issuance of "Product" Brief By Marketing Department	17	94.44	10	90.90	8	100.00	3	60.00	5	100.00
2.	Existence of Customer Complaint System	16	88.88	9	81.81	7	87.5	3	60.00	3	60.00
3.	Availability of Written And Approved Procedure For Sampling	17	94.44	11	100.00	8	100.00	4	80.00	5	100.00
4.	Internal Laboratory Facilities	18	100.00	11	100.00	8	100.00	4	80.00	4	80.00

Type I = Engineering,
Type II = Pharmaceutical & Chemical,
Type III = Electrical & Electronics,
Type IV = Agrobased,
Type V = Textiles

customer-complaint system is reported to be practiced by relatively less number of small organisations. This again might be due to the smaller market size and relative lack of competition.

INSPECTION RELATED PRACTICES

Some inspection related practices have been listed and the respondents were asked to mark either 'Yes/No' against each practice depending upon the presence/absence of that practice.

Size Wise

Results of this analysis are depicted in table 5.13 which is given below :

Table 5.13 Inspection Related Practices : Size Wise

S. No.	Practices	Large Size (Total No.=21)		Small Size (Total No.=26)	
		Number of Organisations	% of Total	Number of Organisations	% of Total
1.	Existence oflist of approved specifications for product and purchased material	19	90.47	25	96.15
2.	Existence of Quality Mannual	18	85.71	19	73.07
3.	Inspection of raw material compulsory before it's release	20	95.23	25	96.15
4.	Inspection of finished goods before it's release	18	85.71	23	88.46
5.	Maintenance of quality document	19	90.47	26	100.00
6.	Identification of defective products	20	95.71	25	96.15
7.	Quarantine of defective products	17	80.95	18	69.23
8.	Reinspection of salvaged products	18	85.71	23	88.46

Organisations in both large (80%) and small (69%) size category devote relatively less attention to 'Quarantine of Defective Products'. Relatively less number of small organisations report the existence of 'Quality Manual'. All other inspection related practices are reported by majority of the respondents.

Age Wise

Inspection related practices have been studied with respect to age of organisations and results are shown in table 5.14.

Table 5.14 Inspection Related Practices : Age Wise

S. No.	Practices	New Companies (Total No.=18)		Old Companies (Total No.=27)	
		Number of Organisations	% of Total	Number of Organisations	% of Total
1.	Existence oflist of approved specifications for product and purchased material	17	94.44	25	92.59
2.	Existence of Quality Mannual	16	88.88	20	74.07
3.	Inspection of raw material compulsory before it's release	17	94.44	26	96.29
4.	Inspection of finished goods before it's release	17	94.44	23	85.18
5.	Maintenance of quality document	16	88.88	27	100.00
6.	Identification of defective products	17	94.44	26	96.29
7.	Quarantine of defective products	15	83.33	18	66.66
8.	Reinspection of salvaged products	16	88.88	23	85.18

The results show almost the same pattern as was observed in case of size wise category. It might be due to the fact that inspection related practices are applicable across age and size of organisations.

Table 5.15 Inspection Related Practices : Type Wise

S. No.	Factors	Type I* Total-18		Type II* Total-11		Type III* Total-08		Type IV* Total-05		Type V* Total-05	
		No.	%	No.	%	No.	%	No.	%	No.	%
1.	Existence of list of approved specifications for product and purchased material	18	100.00	10	90.90	8	100.00	4	80.00	4	80.00
2.	Existence of Quality Mannual	16	88.88	9	81.81	6	75.00	3	60.00	3	60.00
3.	Inspection of raw material compulsory before it's release	17	94.44	11	100.00	8	100.00	4	80.00	5	100.00
4.	Inspection of finished goods before it's release	17	94.44	10	90.90	8	100.00	3	60.00	3	60.00
5.	Maintenance of quality document	17	94.44	11	100.00	8	100.00	5	100.00	4	80.00
6.	Identification of defective products	18	100.00	11	100.00	8	100.00	4	80.00	4	80.00
7.	Quarantine of defective products	13	72.22	10	90.90	7	87.50	2	40.00	3	60.00
8.	Reinspection of salvaged products	17	94.44	10	90.90	7	87.50	3	60.00	4	80.00

Type I = Engineering,
Type II = Pharmaceutical & Chemical,
Type III = Electrical & Electronics,
Type IV = Agrobased, Type V = Textiles

Type Wise

The effects of type wise variations on inspection related practices are depicted in table 5.15. (Pls. see table on the next page)

In Engineering type of industry less respondents reported the practice of 'Quarantine of Defective Products'. All other industries report higher level of inspection related practices.

In some of the organisations separate area is not ear-marked for isolating the defective products and work-in-process materials. Other than this practice all the organisations report relatively same level of inspection related practices.

REFERENCES

Groocock, J.M., 1974. The Cost of Quality, London, Pitman Publishing, pp. 30 - 45. Raju, S.M. Sundara, 1987. "Quality & Top Management", Productivity, Vol 27, No. 4, pp. 377 - 380..pa

CHAPTER 6

PERSPECTIVES ON QUALITY MANAGEMENT PRACTICES

In view of the preceding discussion following perspectives have been developed on improvement of Quality Management Practices in Indian Manufacturing Organisations. In the new economic age no organisation can survive with commonly accepted levels of delays, mistakes, defective materials and defective workmanship. The total cost to produce and dispose of a defective item exceeds the cost to produce a good one. The time has come to shift emphasis from inspection to prevention i.e. the development of a quality assurance system. Rather than having large number of suppliers, it is better to have few dependable suppliers who can meet the quality, price and schedule objectives. The importance of team approach to management should be underlined by means of better coordination among all the functional divisions. Modern methods of education and training of workers, supervisors and departmental heads should be devised and implemented. Expenses on quality should be viewed as investment which in turn will yield returns. The Quality improvement is not possible through inspection alone but will result from the improvement of the process as a whole.

The interpretation of results of analysis reveal that average respondent is about 38 years old, mainly having the designation of Manager/Sr.Manager with engineering background, working in quality department of a manufacturing organisation; work experience ranging from 6 to 10 years. Majority of the organisations are having continuous type of production process, operating on three shifts basis. Relatively more organisations in the sample are of small size, older and engineering type.

The average Quality Management Practice Score is 128 for the sample The results indicate that some confidence is generated in the validity of QMPI instrument developed, on the basis of positive and significant correlation between Quality Management Practice Score and respondent's perception of overall effectiveness of quality department.

In the sample organisation, the statement "The extent to which management assumes responsibility for quality control programme", has emerged at the top with highest mean score. It indicates that in these organisations, the respondents seem to be more than satisfied with responsibility assumed by their top management and as such their support to the quality programmes in the organisations. To the extent the academicians have reiterated time and again in their writings that top management support is essential for the success of any quality management programme - this finding seems to place the practice, in this respect at a very commendable position. Atleast, one can not say that top management is indifferent to the quality aspects in their organisations.

However, contrasting situation has emerged with respect to the factor "Employee Relations" which is at the bottom of the rankings. The general condition in Indian organisations is that the Industrial Relations and Human Resource Development aspects are still being given less attention. Finding of this study supports the same general perceived contention. To improve this situation, more efforts should be given to building of employee relations in general and quality department in particular. The employees should be recognised and rewarded for superior quality performance. Culture of mutual trust should prevail.

ORGANISATION'S CHARACTERISTICS AND QUALITY MANAGEMENT PRACTICES

The small and large size organisations show a significant difference with respect to following factors of quality management : "Training of Employees", "Product Design" and "Quality Data".

As expected, the large companies provide comparatively better training to their employees, better practices relating to product design activities and more systematic management of quality data. It is quite possible that the practices relating to product design may not be applicable to comparatively small organisations. But training of employees and generation & analysis of quality data are equally relevant and applicable to any manufacturing organisation irrespective of size. Therefore it becomes prudent for small organisations, as a matter of fact for all organisations, that they improve practice in respect of these aspects, if at all they are interested in quality development. For the other factors of quality management such as "Role of Quality Department" and "Role of Management" both large and small organisations are reporting higher levels of practices. But, in respect of "Employee Relations" and "Inspection" both large and small sized organisations need to improve their level of practices.

The old and new organisations differ significantly with respect to "Product Design" only. The impact of market competition has been realised more during the last 10 years. World-wide, the competitive organisations have always been coming out with frequent product design changes and new brands and models. Perhaps, that is why the new organisations are attuned to these new philosophies due to the presence of competition. Old organisations, on the other hand, have not been able to overcome inertia. If at all these organisations are willing to take up competition and survive they must revamp their practices, immediately or as a long term strategy. Some complacency seems to have set in old organisations which should be overcome more so, in the wake of emerging situations.

Due to foreign collaborations the new organisations were expected to provide higher amount of training to their employees. Although they are rated as better than old organisations, in this regard, the difference is not large enough to be significant.

Most of the new organisations are launched by new breed of entrepreneurs who are relatively younger, more professionally qualified, and their level of awareness is high. Their attitude is reflected in practices of the new organisations. These organisations are supposed to be having more sophisticated technology due to foreign collaborations, which results in better inspection related practices being reported by these new organisations. Older organisations will also have to pay more attention to inspection related practices even if their processes are not that much sophisticated. Any how, they would have to go in for technological upgradation to face the ensuing competition and any home work done towards this aspect of "Inspection" is likely to benefit in their subsequent efforts.

The size of organisations was found to be dependent on the levels of QMPI but the age of organisations was independent of levels of QMPI. This finding consolidates the result that large organisations differ significantly from small organisations with respect to three factors of Quality Management, as described earlier. Age is not such a significant factor, i.e. if both new and old organisations have to survive their level of Quality Management Practices must improve. However in large organisations the risk of failure is high so they are expected to make more efforts in this respect, in order to survive and prosper - this particular attitude seems to be reflected in the findings of this study in the shape of significant difference emerged between large and small organisations.

ORGANISATIONAL ENVIRONMENT AND QUALITY MANAGEMENT PRACTICES

In many organisations quality Managers are reporting to the managers other than top management. This trend was visible more so in the large organisations. It would be plausible to recommend that in the large organisations also the quality managers should have access to the top management. It will result in increased autonomy for the quality department. For achieving this top management should suitably modify the organisational structure. It is generally recommended in literature that the importance of line relationships of quality management department should be repeatedly highlighted. In the sample, quite many organisations need to look into their organisational structure in such a way that the operations of quality department should not be subordinated under production department. If possible they should be reporting to the top management directly.

Practices like "documentation of lost time" and "availability of trouble shooting list" are receiving less attention of managers in the sample organisations. Documentation of lost time should help in down - time analysis, productivity measurement, and working out cost of quality. For achieving this, documentation system, formats, and reporting practices should be suitably amended.

Quality manual exists for relatively less number of small and old organisations. They should initiate efforts for preparing and implementing quality manual. If quality manual is prepared and meticulously adhered to, it will result in improved quality management practices.

The existence of customer-complaint-system is reported to be practiced by relatively less number of organisations. They would do well to initiate and establish such systems as it will not only improve the quality of their products but will also result in increased customer satisfaction. This should act as a mechanism of customer feedback on a long term basis and help the organisations to frequently review their own operations.

The small organisations do not give due attention to arranging for the "quarantine of defective products", i.e., separate area is not ear-marked to isolate non conforming products. Wherever applicable this practice should be adopted, otherwise the probability of mix-up at delivery stage and consequent rejections from the customer's end may be high.

In Madhya Pradesh, the reported Quality Management Practices adopted by majority of the respondent organisations are satisfactory. The awareness about international standards like ISO 9000 series is increasing. While some organisations have been certified ISO 9000 accreditation, many more organisations are on the way to attaining it. This certification triggers off a chain reaction as the Quality Management Practices followed by suppliers to ISO 9000 companies must also improve. It has become one of the main catalyst for improvement in the Quality Management Practices.

IMPROVEMENT OF QUALITY MANAGEMENT PRACTICES A MACRO LEVEL VIEW POINT

In the light of this study the author has developed a macro level view point for all round improvement of Quality Management Practices in Indian Manufacturing Organisations. In this regard, implementation of following suggestions will be helpful

1. In business organisations, the 'production culture' should give way to 'quality culture'. That culture should be promoted which is based on mutual trust, free and fair exchange of ideas and is focussed on problem solving.
2. The management should develop a quality policy orientation. A quality manual should be prepared to implement the quality policy.
3. The quality management practices are management driven. Commitment for quality should start at the top and this attitudinal change should percolate down to the workers level. The philosophy of "Quality Right First Time and Always" should be followed by management.
4. Expenditure on quality control should not be considered as avoidable expenditure.
5. Total involvement of every person in the organisation is an essential pre-requisite for quality improvement.
6. Inter-departmental coordination and communication system should be improved.
7. Adequate attention should be given to build up Quality Information System as a component of Management Information System of an organisation.
8. Both Quality Control and Production department should not have a common higher authority so that the quality goals are not over-powered. It has also emerged as one of the findings of the study.

9. Training of employees should receive more attention of the top management. The workers in the quality department should be given advanced training in measurement techniques and instrumentations. Follow-up programme to training should be devised to improve effectiveness of such training programmes.
10. Respondents feel that existence of a quality auditing system would act as a catalyst in the right direction.
11. Frequent process and design review activities will result in cost reduction and improved quality of the products.
12. Efforts should be made to increase quality awareness among consumers, this in turn will automatically reflect in the operations of manufacturing organisations.

QUALITY MANAGEMENT RESEARCH : FUTURE PROSPECTS

In the present study an attempt has been made to fill some of the existing knowledge gaps, identified during review of literature. However, it is difficult to expect that a single study would do adequate justice to all aspects. Some suggestions are offered to stimulate thinking to pursue future researches :

1. The geographical coverage of the study may be extended to include organisations located outside Madhya Pradesh.
2. A study of quality related aspects in service organisations may also be undertaken. The quality of services is receiving increased attention now-a-days.
3. The effect of entry of multi national corporationson quality management practices of domestic organisations can be studied, as level of competition influences quality management practices.
4. Influence of various factors such as type of production process, patterns of ownership and management styles on quality management practices can be studied.
5. Organisational structure of quality management and its location in overall organisational structure can be a good area for further research.

6. Industry specific studies may be conducted to determine the prevalent Quality Management Practices.
7. The effect of automation, computerisation and robotics on quality management activities can also be studied.
8. Quality Management Practices of export oriented units can be taken up for future study. This study will be more relevant in the light of commerce ministry's proposal to penalize exporters of sub standard quality goods.
9. Some case studies on implementation of ISO 9000 series type of quality assurance models can be considered for future research.
10. In the present study an instrument has been developed to measure the prevalent Quality Management Practices of an organisation. It needs further refinement. Future empirical researches may be conducted to validate or review this instrument.

SELECT BIBLIOGRAPHY

Ali, A., 1993. "Total Quality Management". Indian Management, Feb.- March.

Allen, Neal and Oakland, J.S., 1988. "Quality Assurance in the Textile Industry : Part I". International Journal of Quality and Reliability Management, Vol. 5, Iss. 5.

Allen, Neal and Oakland, J.S., 1991a. "Quality Assurance in the Textile Industry : Part II". International Journal of Quality and Reliability Management, Vol. 8, Iss. 1.

Allen, Neal and Oakland, J.S., 1991b. "Quality Assurance in the Textile Industry : Part III". International Journal of Quality and Reliability Management, Vol. 8, Iss. 2.American Society for Quality Control, 1986. Principles of Quality Costs. Milwauke : American Society for Quality Control.

Arumugham, P.N., 1986. "The Progress of Quality Management Strategies". In National Conference on Quality. New Delhi, National Productivity Council.

Arumugham, P.N. and Datey, G.W., 1988. A national Strategy for Quality Upgradation. ISI Bulletin, 38 (1).

Asokan, R., 1983. "Quality Circles - The Magic Lamp of Japanese Success Comes to India". Business India, 143, Aug 22-Sept, 11.

Balachandran, K.R. and Srinidhi, B.I.N., 1991. "Target Analysis-Cost, Quality or both". Vikalpa, 16(2), April-June.

Berger, Roger, W. and Shores, David I., 1986. Quality Circles Selected Readings. New York : Marcel Dekker.

Berry, Thomas, H. 1991. Managing Total Quality Transformation. New York : Mc Graw-Hill.

Bureau of Indian Standards, 1988. Quality Assurance System. New Delhi.

Chakraborty, S. 1993. "Is Indian Management Really Committed to Quality". Indian Management, Vol. 32, No. 2 & 3, February-March.

Chandna, J.K., 1992. "Will Total Quality Management succeed in India ?" The Economic Times, November 19.

Chatterjee, P.K., 1993. "Quality Excellence for Productivity Improvement". Productivity, Vol. 34, No. 2, Jul-Sept.

Chaudhuri, K.K., 1985. "Quality Circles-Way of Enhancing Employee Participation". Indian Journal of Industrial Relations, 21 (3).

Crosby, P.B., 1979. Quality is Free. New York : Mc Graw-Hill.

Crosby, P.B., 1984. Quality Without Tears. New York : Mc Graw - Hill.

Crosby, Philip B., 1989. Let's talk quality - 96 questions you always wanted to ask Philip B. Crosby. New York, Mc Graw - Hill.

Datta, Majumdar, B.K. 1987. "Creating Quality Consciousness". Productivity, 27 (4), Jan-Mar.

Deming, W.E., 1981. "Improvement of Quality and Productivity through Action by Management". National Productivity Review. 1 (1).

Deming, W.E., 1986. Out of the Crisis. Cambridge and Posotion MIT, Centre for Advanced Engineering Study.

Deming, W.E., 1986. "What Hapened in Japan ?" In International Conference on Quality. New Delhi, National Productivity Council.

Dutta, P.K., 1985. "Management of Quality - Concepts and Practices in Philips India". QR Journal, 12 (3).

Dwivedi, R.S., 1987. "Effectiveness of Quality Circles and its Determinants in a Large Industrial Organisation in India". Indian Journal of Industrial Relation, 22 (4).

Edosomwan, Johnsonaimie, 1987. Integrating Productivity and Quality Management. New York : Marcel Dekker.

Feigenbaum, Armand V., 1986. "Quality the Strategic Business Imperative". Quality Progress.

Feigenbaum, Armand V., 1983. Total Quality Control. New York McGraw - Hill.

Garvin, David A., 1987. "Competing on the Eight Dimensions of Quality". Harvard Business Review, 87 (6).

Garvin, David, 1983. "Quality on Line". Harvard Business Review, Sept-Oct.

Ghosh, S. and Vihari, V., 1994. "Technology, Quality and Productivity" in Gupta, N.K. and Ahmad, A. (Eds.) Managing Transition, New Delhi : Wiley Eastern Ltd.Hagan, J.T., 1986. Principles of Quality Costs. Wisconsin : ASQC Quality Press.

Harrington, H. James, 1987. The Improvement Process - How America's Leading Companies Improve Quality and Productivity. New York : McGraw - Hill.

Ingle, Sud, 1982. Quality Circles Master Guide. Englewood : Prentice Hal. Irani, J.J., 1987. "Attitude - The key to quality". Productivity, 27 (4), Jan-March.

Ishikawa, Kauro, 1986. "How to Apply the Companywide Quality Control in Foreign Countries". In National Conference on Quality. New Delhi, National Productivity Council, Nov.

Ishikawa, Kauro, 1985. What is Total Quality Control ? The Japanese Way. Englewood : Prentice Hall.

Juran, J.M., 1989. Juran on Leadership for Quality. New York: Free Press. Juran, J.M. and Gryna, Frank, M., 1980. Quality Planning and Analysis. New York : Mc Graw - Hill.

Kaul, Deepak, Dhar, Opinder and Pathak, R.D., 1990. "Quality Circles- Gateway to Worker's Participation" Productivity 31 (3).

Macdonald, J. and Piggott, J., 1992. Global Quality The New Management Culture, New Delhi : Viva Books Pvt. Ltd.

Main, Jermey, 1986. "Under the Spell of the Quality Gurus" Fortune, Aug 18.

Majumdar, D.C., 1987. "Managing Marine Products Quality" Productivity, 27 (4), Jan-March.

Mann, N.R., 1992. The Keys to Excellence - The Deming Philosophy, New Delhi : Viva Books Pvt. Ltd.

Milakevich, Michele, 1990. "Enhancing the Quality and Productivity of State and Local Government". National Civil Review. 79 (3).

Milakovich, Michel, E., 1991. "Total Quality Management in the Public Sector". National Productivity Review. 19 (2), Spring.

Murthy, M.N., 1989. Excellence through Quality and Reliability. Madras : Applied Statistics Centre.

Nandi, S.N., 1988. "Implementing Quality Control Circles in India". Productivity, 28 (4), Jan-March.

Nandi, S.N., 1986. "A Conceptual Model for Effective Working of QC Circles in Indian Context". Lok Udyog, 19 (1).

Nemoto, Masao, 1987. Total Quality Control for Management. London : Prentice Hall.

Oaklad, J.S., 1989. Total Quality Management. Oxford : Heineman.

Paramesvar, K.R., 1986. "Quality Assurance and Quality Management - The Role of Industry". Economic Trends, 15 (23), Dec 1.

Paramesvar, K.R., 1993. "Role of Standards in Technology Management". Productivity, Vol. 33, No. 4, Jan-March.

Rahman, Shams, U.R., 1990a. "Increasing Productivity - The Quality Circle Way". Productivity. 31 (2).

Rahman, Shama, U.R., 1990b. "Management of Service Quality-A Conceptual Frame Work". Productivity, 31 (1). Raju, M.M. Sundara, 1987. "Quality and Top Management". Productivity, 27 (4), Jan - March.

Ross, P.J., 1988. Taguchi Techniques for Quality Engineering. New York : McGraw Hill. Sahu, K.C., 1987. "Quality - Changing Concept and Scope". Productivity. 28 (1), Ap-June.

Samat, B.S., 1987. "Quality Management in an Indian Engineering Enterprise". Productivity. 27 (4), Jan-March.

Scherkenbach, W.W., 1992. The Deming Routeto Quality and Productivity - Road Maps and Road Blocks, New Delhi: Viva Books Pvt. Ltd.Shah, Manubhai, 1987. "Consumer and Quality". Productivity 27 (4), Jan-March.

Sharad, D., 1993. "Total Quality Management Through MBP" Indian Management, Feb. - March.

Sharma, I.M. and R.S. Gupta, 1991. "TQM in Samtel Color Ltd." Productivity, Vol. 32, No. 3, October-December.Shekar, R., 1991. "Modi Xerox Implementation Process Strategy and Elements" Productivity, Vol. 32, No.3, October-December.

Sherkenbach, William, W., 1986. The Deming Route to Quality and Productivity. Washington : CEEP.

Shetty, Y.K. and Buechler Vernon, M., 1988. Competing through Productivity and Quality. Cambridge : Productivity Press.

Singh, Ajit, 1989. "Status of Quality Circles in India". Productivity. 29 (4), Jan-March. Singh, A., 1991. "Total Quality Management : Concept and Practice in India". Productivity, Vol. 32, No.3, October-December.

Singh, A. 1993a. "Quality & the Competitive Environment". Productivity, Vol. 34, No.3, October-December.

Singh, A. 1993b. "Corporate Vision and Quality Policy : Creating an organisation culture". Productivity, Vol. 33, No. 4, Jan-March.

Singh, B., 1993. "Transformational Leadership". Economic Times, New Delhi : December 21.

Sink, D. Scott, 1990. "Total Quality Management is...". Quality and Productivity Management, 8 (2).

Srinivasan, A.V., 1991. "Quality Circle movement in India : A status report". ASCI Journal of Management, Vol. 21, No. 1, June.Sriram, K.S., 1987. "Quality in Small Sector". Productivity, 27 (4), Jan-March.

Sullivan, L.P., 1986. "Quality Function Deployment". Quality Progress, June.

Udpa, S.R., 1982. "Quality Circles Comes to India". OR Journal. 9 (2).

Walton, M., 1986. The Deming Management Method. Milwaukee : Quality Press.

Walton, M., 1993a. The Deming Management Method - The Complete Guide to Quality Management, New Delhi : Viva Books Pvt. Ltd.

Walton, M. 1993b. Deming Management At Work, New Delhi : Viva Books Pvt. Ltd.

Walsh, Loren and Others, 1986. Quality Management Handbook. New York : Marcel Dekker.

Willborn, Walter, 1989. Quality Management Systems. New York, Industrial Press.

Wolf, C. and Hurtado, Y.C., 1990. "Quality Management Practice in Capital Projects". A.A.C.E. Transations.

----, 1994. "Quality Management Centre". University News, September 12.

Young, John, A., 1985. "The Quality Focus at Hewlett - Packard". Journal of Business Strategy, 5 (3), Winter.

APPENDIX A
QUESTIONNAIRE

PART A

Particulars of the person furnishing information.

1. Name --

2. Designation --

3 (a). Name and address of the organization in which serving | ---------------------------- | ---------------------------- | ----------------------------

(b). Year of establishment of the organization | ----------------------------

4. Specific area where you work. (Please tick ( ) one of the following)

   (a) Production planning and control
   (b) Purchase
   (c) Stores
   (d) Process development
   (e) Product development
   (f) Production
   (g) Quality control
   (h) Maintenance, Plant and equipment
   (i) Research and development.

In case you are working in two or more areas, please tick all of them.

5. Please give your age in years ------------------------

6. Educational qualifications ---------------------------
----

7. Professional experience in years ---------------------

PART B

Particulars of the organizations.

1. Whether your organization is :
   Please tick in the appropriate bracket.
   Single plant ... Yes No
   Multiple plant ... Yes No
2. Please name the major products of your organization (in the previous year)

		Rated capacity	Achieved capacity
1.	------------------	------------	----------------
2.	------------------	------------	----------------
3.	------------------	------------	----------------
4.	------------------	------------	----------------

3. Appropriate total sales turn over of your company for the last three years.
   1990 - 91 --------------------------
   1991 - 92 --------------------------
   1992 - 93 --------------------------
4. Which of the following standard/s is/are applicable for your organization ?
   (a) I.S.O. 9000
   (b) B.I.S. (I.S.I.)
   (c) AGMARK
   (d) Any other (please specify)
5. Whether the planning and execution for obtaining cer tification for the above standard/s is at :
   (a) Initial stage.
   (b) Advanced stage.
   (c) Nearing completion.
   (d) Certified.
   (e) Not applicable.lh8
6. Total number of employees.
   (a) Managerial level ----------------------
   (b) Supervisory level ----------------------
   (e) Others ----------------------

7. Whether the production is :
   (a) On job order basis
   (b) Batch production
   (c) Continuous production
   (d) Assembly line
8. Number of shifts generally worked.
   One two three
9. Please list the departments in the production area.
   1. 2.
   3. 4.
   5. 6.
   7. 8.

   Of the above departments which three departments are comparatively important in the organization ? Please list them below in order of importance.

   1. ------------------------------------
   2. ------------------------------------
   3. ------------------------------------

   If there is no separate Quality Control Department, please indicate below which among the existing depart ment looks after quality control.

PART C

Please use the scale given below to evaluate each item.

"Extent of prevailing practice" is :

Non applicable Very low Low Medium High Very High Letter

Code A B C D E F

Subsequently this scale will be given only by its letter code for sake of brevity. You are requested to consider the prevailing situation carefully before **marking a tick** ( ) in the appropriate column of the above scale.

	Please mark tick A B C D E F
(1) The extent to which top management/ functional man agement owns responsibility for quality control programme.	
(2) Specificity of quality goals.	
(3) Efforts to develop and publish quality policy.	
(4) Extent to which quality goals/ policy are understood by the employees.	
(5) Importance given to quality by management in relation to cost and schedule objectives.	
(6) Visibility/identity of the quality department.	
(7) Quality department access to the top management.	
(8) Autonomy of the quality department.	
(9) Coordination between the quality department and other departments.	
(10) Effectiveness of the quality dep- artment in improving and maintaining quality.	

"Extent of prevailing practice" is :

Non applicable Very low Low Medium High Very High

Code A B C D E F

Please mark tick

A B C D E F

(11) Quality related training given to the employees of :
(a) Production Department
(b) Quality Department
(c) Other Departments.

(12) Advanced training given to the workers of quality department.

(13) Training in the basic statistical techniques (such as sampling, dispersion etc.) to the employees of quality department.

(14) Availability of resources for employee training.

(15) Effectiveness of training programs for improving the skills of employees.

(16) Thoroughness of new product design before the product is produced and marketed.

(17) Frequency of updating design activities as the design evolves.

(18) Coordination among various concerned departments in the product development process.

(19) Clarity of product specifications and procedures.

(20) Extent to which implementation and existing process capabilities are considered in the product design process.

(21) Extent to which product is identified throughout all the stages of production, delivery and installation

(22) Extent to which the selection of suppliers/subcontractors is based on quality criteria.

"Extent of prevailing practice" is :

Code	Non applicable	Very low	Low	Medium	High	Very High
	A	B	C	D	E	F

Please mark tick
A B C D E F

(23) Thoroughness of supplier rating system.

(24) Reliance on few dependable suppliers.

(25) Use of statistical control charts.

(26) Amount of preventive equipment maintenance.

(27) Extent to which process design minimizes probability of employee error.

(28) Use of acceptance sampling.

(29) Importance of Inspection review or checking of work.

(30) Availability of quality data.

(31) Timeliness of quality data.

(32) Extent to which quality data are used as a tool to manage quality.

(33) Extent to which quality slogans and information about quality data and control charts are displayed at work stations.

(34) Extent to which quality circles or other employee involvement type programs are implemented in plant.

(35) Effectiveness of quality circles or other employee involvement type programs.

(36) Extent to which employees are recognized for superuor quality performance.

(37) Extent to which workers participate in quality decisions.

APPENDIX D

RESULTS OF F-ANOVA TEST

Table D.1 : Between types of Industries for "Aggregate Quality Management Practices"

Source	S.S.	d.f.	M.S.	F
Between types	1266.00	4	316.49923	0.33
Error	40284.98	42	959.16623	
Total	41550.98	46		

Table D.2 : Between types of Industries for "Role of Management"

Source	S.S.	d.f.	M.S.	F
Between types	57.84	4	14.46006	0.54
Error	1117.86	42	26.61576	
Total	1175.70	46		

Table D.3 : Between types of Industries for "Role of Quality Department"

Source	S.S.	d.f.	M.S.	F
Between types	13.29	4	3.32257	0.17
Error	806.92	42	19.21244	
Total	820.21	46		

Table D.4 : Between types of Industries for "Training of Employees"

Source	S.S.	d.f.	M.S.	F
Between types	87.41	4	21.85319	0.38
Error	2428.46	42	57.82047	
Total	2515.87	46		

Table D.5 : Between types of Industries for "Product Design"

Source	S.S.	d.f.	M.S.	F
Between types	56.23	4	14.05852	0.34
Error	1739.68	42	41.42097	
Total	1795.91	46		

Table D.6 : Between types of Industries for "Supplier Quality Management"

Source	S.S.	d.f.	M.S.	F
Between types	21.57	4	5.39303	0.59
Error	384.08	42	9.14476	
Total	405.65	46		

Table D.7 : Between types of Industries for "Inspection"

Source	S.S.	d.f.	M.S.	F
Between types	64.58	4	16.14620	0.85
Error	796.82	42	18.97189	
Total	861.40	46		

Table D.8 : Between types of Industries for "Quality Data"

Source	S.S.	d.f.	M.S.	F
Between types	21.89	4	5.47127	0.34
Error	667.86	42	15.90142	
Total	689.74	46		

Table D.9 : Between types of Industries for "Employee Relation"

Source	S.S.	d.f.	M.S.	F
Between types	76.49	4	19.12331	1.03
Error	776.31	42	18.48360	
Total	852.80	46		